SMOL HEALINGS

THE SLOW ART OF CARING FOR YOUR INNER WORLD

KRISHNAN S

Clever Fox® PUBLISHING
Chennai • Bangalore

CLEVER FOX PUBLISHING
Chennai, India

Published by CLEVER FOX PUBLISHING 2025

ISBN: 978-93-6707-920-1

"Dayardra Himagiri Thanaye,
ease our long journey"

CONTENTS

INTRODUCTION

The crescent moon shines through my window as I begin to write these pages. Slender and warm, the shadow seems cradled by it. The sound of distant vehicles, dogs barking, and crickets fills the air. The lights are dim and call out for sleep. It smells of some preparation from downstairs. I am feeling nervous, gripped by the uncertainty of the blank page. I gulp some water and let my muscles relax, opening myself up to the process. It feels easier as the words pop up on the page. Life seems to be an unceasing flow of perturbations to stabilize, and seeking a sense of stability and wholeness is what we yearn for. That covers the poetry requirements for this chapter.

Welcome to this short booklet, a take on mental health and the path to healing shaped as I have walked it. This book is meant to be a companion, something you can carry around and learn about the various ways to foster mental well-being, discover healing, challenge concepts, review and broaden, and most importantly, practice and integrate into your life. By going through the book, you will hopefully gain an appreciation for the tools that work (for me) when in a tough situation, and be able to make sense of it for your own journey.

If you are a seasoned practitioner, may this serve as a reminder. If you're here out of curiosity, then may this book captivate your interest. If you're here out of pain, maybe loneliness, then I hope that this book will hold space for you. I see your struggle, and I wrote this book especially for you, somebody who just needs a friendly, caring book to talk to them. I hope that this book serves a purpose, whatever way of life you come from. Try to take it in a warm, gentle, and slow tone; you can imagine I'm a little, fuzzy creature.

I absorbed most of my learnings about mental health in my young adult years, particularly with fervour since 2023, following a heavy depressive episode where I once again had no hope left, echoes of a troubled childhood. I didn't know what to do at the time, and I randomly picked a psychiatrist off a listing website and visited him as soon as I could. That led me to get psychometrically tested, and I met my wonderful therapist. Without going into details, it was a very enriching process, where I learned intensely both in and out of therapy in a determination to overcome my challenges. The road is long, however, and there is much yet to heal, but the experiences granted much knowledge and insight. Out of a natural need, I felt it necessary to help other people through their bumpy journeys as well, having a strong mother archetype in me, and hoarding what is essentially sacred knowledge. I have come to be a connoisseur of practices for mental well-being. Working directly with people was not in the cards, so I hypothesized that I would write this book so that it may help someone else in their own unfolding process. Let me be of service to you in this regard.

This book is split into five sections, each one focusing on a particular aspect of healing, starting from gaining a sense of emotional grounding and safety so that the day to day is a little easier, followed by introspection to really understand ourselves, our needs, and then expression, to further our internal study and honor ourselves in ritual. The aim is to cultivate a basic understanding of each aspect and have some integrative practices to follow. These five sections speak on presence, kindness, clarity, creativity, and the inner world, respectively. Although there may be more categories, I find that these will cover, hopefully, what is needed. Feel free to skip, but keep in mind I've tried to keep these in order of immediacy. The earlier chapters will help with coping, whereas the later ones are on deeper identification of yourself and your patterns. If you go in the opposite direction, you may find yourself overwhelmed. Also ideas that you learn in earlier chapters will add richness to ideas that come later, which you may not pick up on if reading out of order.

I draw my material from various sources, so I will try to mention what books and websites have helped me shape my collection. There is a tiny bibliography at the end if you would like to peruse it earlier.

Having read this far, consider your mental well-being as of this moment; are you fatigued? Lack of sleep? Irritated, sad? Lethargic, bed rotting? Worried, fearful? Lack of life energy? Overwhelmed? Or maybe just okay, peaceful? Thriving? Keep a track of how you feel as you progress through the book, and see if you feel any changes by applying the material. It will be good to see if the notes are really helping you; your own experience will be what shows you the efficacy of the techniques. Keep yourself open to the content, be curious towards it as well as your own experience, "How do I feel about this?". If you feel like a part of you is being defiant, ask it to wait for a page or two, and work from there. The unfortunate truth is that there is no magic; you have to do the work, and even though you may be exhausted and broken, there will be a minimal practice you can think of that will wait for you. Hold on, do as little as you can manage; no step is wasted. Imagine the network of healers that have come together to pass on this knowledge to you through me, and be comforted by their loving intentions. If you do feel all fragile and distressed at the start of this book, don't fret. Hopefully, by the later chapters, you will be more stable, holding space for yourself, calm, cool, and curious.

Healing is a spiral. You will revisit concepts and practices again and again, refining them at each point. It doesn't have a deadline either. You may regress at certain points in time, but don't be disheartened; you will have made more progress than regress. It can be really difficult when you end up breaking your sobriety or something. I can't imagine. You may lose hope and beat yourself up mercilessly. But the next moment is there to always hold us, and even though you feel broken, you can find your way again. It is right there to pick off from where you were. You haven't failed. Setbacks are just part of the journey. Analytical psychology talks a lot about wholeness and balance, and sometimes setbacks are just the counterweight you need to move forward, but only if you accept that it is.

Disclaimer: I am not a licensed mental health professional, and what I'm giving you is not professional medical advice, diagnoses, or treatment. The book is about my own experiences with different approaches to healing that have helped me over the years; tools, reflections, and comfort. If you are going through something painful, please seek help from a mental health professional. You can use this book as a companion to walk beside you and hold space, to help keep track of concepts, get a feel for what may be helpful for you, and to discuss the ideas with a therapist to see if they are suitable for your journey.

Additional disclaimer: I also realize that healing may look different for each of us, especially if we come from neurodivergent backgrounds, are queer folks, or have lived in oppression, because the world looks different. What is normal and safe for me may not be safe for you. But perhaps there will be some tools here that give you some space for yourself.

If you currently have to live where it is unsafe, I pray that something helps you out of your circumstances. I know it may not be possible for you to just leave. May this book offer you what little control you can take back of your own life. Your heart is yours alone.

Mimi, the Capybara, gently raises her head to look at you. She takes a few sniffs, tilts her head, and makes a smol noise. She returns to her bowl of oats, gathering the energy she needs to accompany you on this eventful journey through your internal world. She has stickers from all parts of the world; she's a guide of the heart. Be sure to bring some berries and cherries for her to munch on. You two are friends now.

✦✦✦

CHAPTER 1

PRESENCE

This first chapter is going to be about gaining a sense of stability and firmness in your mental and emotional states through various mind-body practices. It is about teaching you to dislodge yourself from a difficult position and return to your center, possibly to build a home in that feeling. Imagine yourself staring out into a pond, and you watch as the choreographed ripples come and go over the still water. The pond always returns to stillness, and the deeper waters hardly stir. That's the kind of imagery that catches the spirit of this chapter.

In our daily lives, we often end up getting carried away by what is boiling inside of us, most times unaware that it is steaming and spouting and making all kinds of noises. We find that our mental and emotional momentum dictate our behaviour and thoughts. For example, when I have presentations to do, I end up becoming quite anxious, and that makes the presentation so much more difficult to do, inviting many unpleasant thoughts such as "Am I making a mess?" or "Do they think I'm stupid?". It's a common thought to have, the modern world traps us in a trance of unworthiness ('Radical Acceptance', Tara Brach). If I take a few minutes to be in presence, disarm the emotion, then things tend to settle, and the presentation goes smoothly. It is a very simple truth that works well in practice: process the emotion, return to peace. It works on all scales. I've been in grief of having lost somebody, a long-lasting grief, and trying to center brought softness to that difficult place, not remove it, but to really be held moment to moment. Of course, it isn't a magic fix-it-all; grief doesn't disappear overnight. Or maybe it will for you. Centering typically takes steady practice, but maybe you're on the cusp of transformation.

The idea of presence, like the word suggests, is to be in the present moment. It is also called awareness, mindfulness, grounding, and sati. It comes in different forms, but the essence of it is to be wholly with yourself, inner and outer environment both, not in the past, not in the future, but now, like catching the eye of a curious crow, two beings locked in recognition. Presence is the practice of paying attention intently, keenly, and possibly lovingly. In that attention, one finds that the system settles; the mind slows down, the emotions mellow out, and the blood pumps without urgency. What is key to awareness is that you are noticing your perceptions, thoughts, and feelings. You are aware that you are thinking, feeling happiness, and observing a round bird. You are able to notice the noticing. This sort of zoomed-out state allows one to look upon things without being consumed by said things. The mind-body feels safe; your parasympathetic nervous system switches on, the system responsible for rest and digest, in response to gentle awareness. Presence is a wonderful way to treat anxiety, as it allows you to cope and settle so that you may examine the roots.

Now that may be all abstract and lofty, so sit with me and try to bring your attention to any one object in your room, and just observe it. Study the color, the texture it may be, its weight, its sturdiness, it may bring up an emotion, multiple thoughts. Every time something comes up and distracts you, and you happen to catch yourself, try to bring your focus back to the object. You may remember a story and start retelling it in your head, but gently bring attention back to the object when you do notice that you have wandered off. After 5-10 minutes, see how you feel. Is there a sense of openness at all, like your brain is more spacious? Do things feel slower, calmer? It's okay if it doesn't feel like much. This is one way to practice presence, and it may be the only one you need to understand it.

This is a gateway into the now, as Eckhart Tolle ('The Power of Now') describes it, and the more you practice, the more you will be able to stay there. Your body will learn to regulate and be safe. In this chapter, I'll detail more gateways, as one may work for you better than others, so it is good to have choices. This is about pacing, regulating your emotions, and handling distress; it is your own first aid kit when the emotional stones are being pelted. However, it also facilitates your self-awareness, "What am I thinking?", "What am I feeling?", which will help you understand yourself better and is a necessary foundation for deeper work, although you may choose not to do deeper work if you wish, no pressure. If you get triggered by a stimulus, that is, you have an adverse reaction to something, you may have developed your mind to be able to notice what triggered you and slow down, and reflect on the situation later if you feel the need. You can notice unhelpful patterns in thought and behaviour and contemplate change. Mindfulness is a two-prong approach: settling and observing. It allows for a pause in reacting to our external and internal, and you have time to think and respond instead of reacting to it without the slightest contemplation.

Don't mistake the idea that being in the now means you forgo the past and future. You still have to live from your past experiences, and plan for future actions, which is part of being a living being. Doing so from a peaceful space makes the time travel a little easier. You can slowly let your baggage go and let down your worries. We will build on this later.

If you have suffered through adverse experiences, have trauma, and/or have not worked with your emotions very deeply, a more external bodily sensation-oriented practice would be better for you, something they refer to as somatic. Techniques that focus on being highly internal may bring up unpleasant memories and emotions, which you will want a therapist/an informed friend around to help you with. In present-day studies, they have shown that meditation, for example, can be deleterious as it can bring up contents from the unconscious mind that you may not be ready for. You may choose to come back to these exercises when you feel better equipped.

Mindfulness can be practiced on various things, like the breath, thoughts, feelings, or external objects. It all comes down to what helps us become anchored in the present moment. There are many ways to do this, and you can use your creativity to design your own methods. Healing is very personal and subjective, so finding your own ways is not a bad thing. A healthy mix of both objective and subjective helps. You can practice most of these methods anywhere; the point is to be able to have access to them whenever you need them, when you are anxious, distressed, or low. It is also potent for dissociation, helping you return from that temporary alternate space back into grounded reality. Dissociation is a defensive mechanism, and it can make you feel comfortable if you've been in it for long, but the full spectrum of life is much desired. Have the gentle courage to step into the realness of life through presence, and you can heal your wounds and overcome your hardship.

By the way, don't be overwhelmed thinking you have to do all the exercises that follow. You need only try a few that you feel pulled towards.

Breathing:

Let us open with a basic meditation practice. Close your eyes and take a deep breath in, one long inhale, and a longer exhale. Give yourself the permission to really rest in this moment, we are slowing on purpose. Every exercise can be as short as you like, but immerse yourself. Bring your attention to your breath; you can focus on the nostrils, the feeling of air in your body, or the movement of your stomach. Take big belly breaths so you can get a feel for it. Then allow yourself to breathe naturally, don't force a rhythm. You can gently think "in" on inhales and "out" on exhales, or maybe 1 and 2. If any thought or emotion comes to you, gently acknowledge it, and bring focus back to your breath. It is natural to have thoughts come and go; the point isn't to have no thoughts. If you find them overwhelming, stop and try a different grounding technique. You can do this exercise for as long as you like. At the end, open your eyes and just sit for a few minutes in presence. You should feel like you've quieted down, but no pressure if not, you may just need practice, or you may benefit from a different way. It's okay if you get lost in your thoughts; it will become easier.

Now, I find that the above may not always be suitable for every case, which is true for any technique. When I'm in a more anxious place, sometimes it can be difficult to rest on the breath—you may feel like it's quick, and it stresses you further. In that case, we turn to a more active approach. We could try box breathing. As before, sit down and settle with a deep breath. Follow the pattern of inhaling through the nose for four seconds, holding for four, exhaling through the mouth for four, and holding for four. Doesn't have to be perfect. Feel the air cycle through you. Repeat that for a few minutes. This deliberately paced active breathing should help calm your system. A variation on this is to inhale through the nose for four seconds, hold for seven, and exhale through the mouth for eight. Shorten the duration if you feel like it's hard.

Mimi pulls on your clothes, asking you to sit down. She props her hand on her stomach and asks you to take big belly breaths. She turns into a rolly polly ball

You can imagine that you're an airbender like Aang from ATLA. You're willing the air element into your body and out to help promote stability in your system. Visualize the flow of air as it circulates, imagine that it softly loves your insides. If you feel like you can, thank the air for providing itself to us.

Don't be hard on yourself if you find something isn't working, and don't dismiss it altogether either. We all come from unique circumstances; it's just a matter of experimenting. This chapter is filled with exercises so you can see what works for you.

Mental Phenomena:

The next practice we could try doing is to watch our internal world, just be a silent spectator. This can bring up things like hard memories, so be careful.

Sit down and close your eyes; this is a recurring theme in meditation. Here, simply wait for a thought or feeling to come; it could be imagery, bodily sensations, music, math, or various mental things. Whenever something comes in, notice it, tell yourself internally that you are noticing a thought or a feeling, "I am noticing this thought about pasta," and don't hold on. Let the next moment come. Let the thoughts and feelings come and go as they like; you stay in the silent backdrop. It's okay if you don't point out every thought or feeling; there may be too many. You may get engaged with a thought - bring yourself back to noticing. It's like you are in a bus depot; a bus rolls up, but you don't get on, you just notice it and watch it leave. Do so for a few minutes. This may sound bizarre for an exercise, but what happens is that it helps with defusion. You start to realise that you are not your thoughts, or your feelings, or even your sensations. You realize it is just a color, klishta, that gets overlayed on you, and it can come and go whenever. Something else is at the core of who you are, the "Self," maybe? You are not anxiety or depression yourself, and if that's true, maybe it's easier to work through them. It should also slow things down. Separating from your emotions a little bit is good to get a good look at your thoughts. You're not pushing away the thought, "I don't want it" types; just stepping back.

If you're finding it hard to feel things, try the body scan exercise that comes up soon. Learn to associate what your body does when you are in certain situations. If your head feels like being smushed in and you want to behave aggressively, you may be angry, defiant. If your chest feels a little empty like it's being pulled in, that's sadness, maybe grief. When you feel full and want to jump around, maybe that's happiness and excitement. It is a process of re-parenting yourself to learn emotions.

A variation on this exercise is to notice how we label our phenomena. We are quick to judge our thoughts and feelings as good or bad, right or wrong, and these are split-second decisions. So the goal is to just let go of that judgment, neither good nor bad; this is just a judgment. Our thoughts and feelings are actors and messengers; they are not inherently evil; they serve a purpose of informing you about something. Your values and actions determine who you are, not your random thoughts. As someone who has OCD, intrusive thoughts are rather commonplace, especially when stressed. This exercise showed me not to take them as damning, and that I don't have to be distressed. Bad things happened to me that generate intense thoughts, but they aren't the be-all and end-all of my life. Thoughts are just thoughts.

On a side note, since we mentioned OCD, being in presence and regulating your emotions is useful when exposure therapy is being employed. It can help you stay centered when you are being exposed to something you want to avoid, like the fear of contamination. The idea is to not run away from your emotions, but to allow them to happen, and presence allows for greater tolerance. Similarly, slowly and compassionately, exposure therapy helps with trauma responses. Exposure therapy takes place in small increments of what you're trying to overcome, but this isn't something you should jump to on your own without help and familiarity. Speak to a therapist about whether it is appropriate for you and what you could do realistically.

It may be a good idea to keep a track of what you notice during your meditation, as it may show you what you need to work on currently. Write down thoughts that you have which make you feel something, especially if they bring down your mood or cause anxiety. Later on, we'll speak on what we can do about these thoughts, but to summarize, really question your thoughts and try to find out if they are true. What is helpful for you?

Mimi didn't realize she had so many thoughts about muffins and strawberries. Maybe we could get some. What is on your mind?

Sensory Experience:

These exercises will be about using our sense perception to bring ourselves into the moment, and are useful for those who have trauma. You can use each sense organ separately as its own exercise, or you can combine them, or do them in order. The most common grounding exercise is the 5-4-3-2-1 exercise. Find yourself in a sitting or standing position. Look around and name five things in your room. Do so slowly and deliberately, move your torso and your neck to look around like you're surveying the scene. You may observe the objects slightly. After that, name four things you can hear, take a couple of seconds. Name three things you can feel, anywhere in your body, and allow yourself to feel the texture. Name two things you can smell, or remember smelling. And name one whatever you can taste. Give attention to each step. By the end, you should feel more centered. The idea is to move your attention to the senses, giving time for your body to settle.

You can make various exercises on your own based on which sense works well for you. Feel is a good one, you can play with a rock or a stick you found and really notice the shapes and textures, roll it around in your hand and feel the weight. You can use temperature as an input; for instance, when stressed, I like making a cup of tea, and I'll gently put my palms on the cup so that it radiates heat into my hands. You slowly sip and let the heat warm you up, and savor the taste. You can use ice cubes, which are good for distressing feelings, and are part of the DBT TIPP distress tolerance mnemonic (Google it). Observe objects like we did earlier in the book. So as you can see, there are multiple ways of going about this.

An exercise I like doing from time to time is to listen past all the sounds in the outside world to get to the silence beneath all of it. It is a tricky exercise, but imagine that you have a blank piece of paper and you drew something on top. Even though the drawing is there, the blank paper is still underneath the ink. Similarly, there's always a silence beneath the sounds. This requires deep focus, so don't do it if it will frustrate you, but once you get it, it's not too difficult to go back. I find the exercise quite profound. You can also look for silence in between noises, which is a bit easier.

Getting into your body is also a good way to ground. You can do the body scan approach, where you start from one end of your body to another, keeping your mind focused on each part. For example, you lie down and you start monitoring your toes for any sensations, you move up your shins to knees, up your thighs to the hips, stomach to chest, chest to arms, arms to hand, hand to fingers, back to shoulders to neck, and your face, to the crown of your head, and at each part pause for a few seconds and notice is what is going on; are there itches, any pain, warm or cool, tingling, buzzing, throbbing, wicky wacky taffiling? Relax your muscles wherever you feel tension. Like in the exercises with thoughts, let the sensations arise and drop, let them come and go, you're safe here. This is a beautiful exercise because you really are giving your whole loving attention to your body, taking a moment to check in with how it is doing, something we neglect. As you practice, you will become more aware of how your body behaves and signals things, like when your diet is not okay, your body feels a certain anxiety.

A good mid-term anxiety reliever is Jacobson's Progressive Muscle Relaxation exercise. It is very similar to the above exercise. You go from one end to the other and tighten your muscles at each part for a few seconds, and release them, inducing relief in that area from having let go of tension. You really have to lean into the relief. Over time, your body learns to relax better. Over the span of two months, I had attended this biofeedback therapy where they would monitor various parameters like my EEG signals and my heart rate, and over time, JPMR showed results; I was calmer. My EEG was always pretty high, but my body was calm. That probably might be because I also had a good rapport with my biofeedback therapist.

Mimi yawns; she's always a little relaxed. That's a safe nervous system. She's got no jaguars to worry about right now.

To round it off, movement is also a good way to invite presence; a dance of the heart, yoga, running shoes on the pavement, or intense calisthenics may be ways to ground yourself. I will speak a little more on these in later chapters. Even slow strolls through your neighborhood are good for your mind, so try to incorporate some walking into your day if you feel called to.

You may also look into vagal nerve stimulation exercises such as "Voo Tuning", or shaking your arms and legs, and bouncing up and down when you're anxious, or butterfly tapping.

Mental Taxation:

Of the different grounding techniques I've mentioned so far, this category is the one that I always find humorous, as you will find yourself tripping into calmer and pleasant inner spaces. The idea is to focus on some kind of a game that takes focus. You may find this frustrating, but try to keep at it. The first way I usually tell other people is to do math. Depending on your computing skills, give yourself arithmetic that you find difficult. For some people, it may just be adding two or three digit numbers, for others it may be multiplication, perhaps even estimating square roots if you're fancy. Do a couple of these sums, and if you really had to tax your brain to calculate, you will find yourself moving towards peace. I once was talking to a friend struggling emotionally about her self-image, burning emotion, and I threw math at her willy-nilly. Thankfully, she was open to the task, and it helped her calm down enough to laugh at the situation.

Another taxing task is to try and recite a poem or a story from memory. For instance, I like recalling "Stopping By Woods On A Snowy Evening" by Robert Frost. Even though I may not actually remember the words, trying to fill them in and repeating parts like a mantra helps you stay in the present moment; "miles to go before I sleep, I have miles to go before I sleep". Similarly, recalling non-triggering facts about your life can be helpful: "I ate an apple, but the skin was weird, maybe they painted it red. How come apples are so expensive? Are they rare?". You could also list items belonging to a category. Back in school, kids would compete with each other in a game called Name-Place-Animal-Thing, and what you would do is that you would list an item from each category in alphabetical order. So for A, you might say Alice, Arizona, Armadillo, and Aubergine. You repeat it for other letters until you feel calmer. You could come up with any other task like this.

Visualization is a powerful tool in many ways. Sit down in a quiet environment and imagine that you are in a safe place inside your head, a place where it is peaceful and happy, maybe like a memory of playing at the beach. Spend some time in that memory, and let the warmth heat up your bones. When you feel okay, you can let go of the image and come back to our reality. I've had times where I've imagined myself pouring buckets of powder into the ocean, signifying that I was letting my worries be eaten up by the cosmos, and that led to a sense of closure. We will be making more use of this technique later, so feel free to try it out and see how you feel about it. Do you find it hard to visualize images? Maybe you can rely on audio or messages, or what sensations are popping up. You can pick up spontaneous moments of safety and wonder, like sunlight coming through the window, and use that memory as an anchor. Deb Dana calls these "glimmers" in her book on Polyvagal Theory in therapy.

Mimi doesn't know what 27 × 45 is, but she can count on her paws. You'll have to help her handle money.

So, at this point, we've covered a large chunk of mindfulness work that you can pick and choose from. The point is to show you the map, and you can choose where to go. You may feel overwhelmed; that's when you throw a dart at the book and try one of the exercises that the dart lands on. Nothing like actual work.

Resistance:

One of the trickiest parts about working with the mind is the unconscious resistance you have against yourself. When you notice a certain unpleasant emotion like anger or sadness, your instinct is to remove it as soon as possible, delete, and disappear. This applies to external objects as well. You are in direct conflict with the emotion or person, or situation, and you may not recognise that layer of resistance unless somebody points it out for you. It is natural to want to avoid unpleasant things. However, seemingly paradoxically, the less you try to remove the feeling or thought, the easier it is to process the emotion.

The unpleasant emotion brings a small weighted bag, and the resistance on top adds several more bags of suffering, "I don't want it, this is unfair, get it away from me, this is your fault, why me?". Fighting the emotion is difficult; it is easier on you if you can drop the resistance and accept the presence of the emotion. It's okay to feel what you feel; it is part of the human experience to feel the full spectrum of emotions. That allows your nervous system to relax, since you're no longer struggling against something. Try to be less judgmental about your feelings; they're not inherently good or bad, they are there to show something. It doesn't mean accepting external harm, but accepting the presence of your inner phenomena.

Towards the end of 2022, I went through some emotional turmoil, and I couldn't go to work anymore. I was quite depressed. On top of that, I started getting crippling anxiety attacks when the sun would go down. I would lie in bed with my eyes closed, waiting for it to get over, but it would take a few hours, and I would eventually fall asleep, thanks to medication. I looked for ways to overcome this. One thing that helped was that I got a cajon and tried playing it loudly when I would get anxious, and it would work briefly, but the anxiety would come back again. Eventually, one night, maybe twenty days into this, something I read clicked, and I just lay down, putting my attention on the anxiety. I let go of the fear by simply watching the anxiety, I stopped struggling and pitying. I focused on the sensation in my body, the place where it was most anxious, and I really zoomed in to understand its shape, was it a line, a circle? And to my relief, the anxiety washed away. I had a tool that I could use, and the attacks stopped happening; it was a real miracle. Later on, I extended this technique by applying it to just about anything you may struggle with by focusing attention on that mental object.

When it comes to being in presence, I find this technique works best for me. Emotions respond well to undivided, non-judgmental attention. Simply look inside and try to recognize and name your emotions, like when you feel empty, for instance. Then think about letting go of a hot stone that you were holding on to too tightly, or a dam that had a shutter open, and let go of any qualms, expectations, or resistances. It's just about releasing that pressure you feel. Then put your attention on the feeling, any sensations in the body, really let the body speak to you. Periodically check if you are resisting, and release if so. In a few minutes, you should see improvement. Be careful, however, the emotion may briefly increase in intensity seemingly before it gets better, and it may be overwhelming. When it gets attention, it wants to be seen. Maybe stick with other techniques for some time so that you know you can switch techniques if it gets too hot. Instead of some of the distracting present-moment techniques we saw, this one asks you to go deep into the problem. There is a variation later in this book that I found that is very similar to the RAIN technique by Tara Brach, and also similar to The Sedona Method by Hale Dwoskin (well, technically, Lester Levenson), in that they all apply this approach of accepting and letting go towards physical sensations.

This is good for panic attacks as well, which happen as a fear-of-fear reaction. If you can suspend the fear by accepting it, the panic attack will die down. Your body is just having a reaction is all.

At the heart of some of these techniques is also the idea of acceptance; to accept a thought, feeling, person, situation, which is love in some ways. It's to allow something to be, as they are, without being overtaken by judgment. Acceptance does not mean resignation to your circumstances; it is about allowing things to exist, liked or disliked, good or bad. You can choose to make decisions from that place of internal non-resistance. It opens up energy that you can use for managing your situation. For example, I am aware that someone I know is going to have opinions I don't necessarily agree with, but I accept that person for who they are, and we can have a conversation that doesn't end up in frustration. Of course, if you feel compelled to change their mind, please speak; it's just that things are clearer from a position of acceptance. Many people do find it difficult to let go of their pain or anger, for reasons such as accountability or preserving memory. And that's okay, whatever your reason, maybe you just want to hold anger against someone for a while, or even against yourself, maybe you're going through grief. It's part of the path. Just ask yourself if you could just be open to the idea of accepting things and see what happens anyway. Maybe it will bring you peace. The more you see it working, the more it will help you when you are in distress.

I would like to say, as a person who grew up with a lot of emotional volatility and explosions, the pause in presence is what really allows you to redirect your emotions. If you have BPD, for example, then the pause is what will help with dysregulation and splitting. If you have brought presence into your life, you will be able to identify at the moment your nervous system is going to erupt, and you can try to take a moment to come down, and maybe change your assumptions about what is happening. Maybe it won't happen the first or second time, but each time you'll know that there are opportunities to pause and regulate, and perhaps take a compassionate approach, as we'll see in the next chapter. I know how it feels to explode, so let's take care of ourselves and practice the pause.

And with that, we come to the end of this chapter. This is already a big step that you are taking in your mental health journey, so thank you for coming this far with me. Practice a few select techniques when you can, and let's see how it changes your day-to-day. We will be building on some of the concepts here in the chapters to come, so having a good foundation is helpful.

Be safe.

You and Mimi have a relaxing time playing in the Meadow Of Settling; you bother all the dragonflies, sit on ancient rocks, nibble on white flowers with squirrels, and play in the burbling brook. Mimi doesn't rush things at all; when she's in the water, she's really soaking in the sun and the water, with carefully balanced oranges on her head. You plod over the grass and feel your feet collect the raw earth. The ground supports you, and the air fills your lungs. You feel your mind slow down, yet enliven. Mimi ticks off activities from her list.

✦✦✦

CHAPTER 2

KINDNESS

This second chapter is about the quality of compassion, particularly self-compassion. It is about treating yourself with kindness, empathy, respect, and love, among other things. This is the process of setting up a water station outside on the balcony or garden of your mind during summer, so that mental birds can come rest and hydrate themselves. It is about welcoming the branches of the sleeping tree to lull you to the dream world, to rest deeply. It is about softly observing, absorbing, and responding. The last chapter taught you how to be with yourself; this one is about caring for yourself from that place.

Most of us reading this book carry wounds from childhood (0-21 years) that colour how we feel about the world and ourselves. We have wounds that broadcast the message that we are not enough; appearances, finances, capability, achievements, romance, and simply just living. If you come from trauma, you may believe you don't deserve to be here. Even though you are putting all your efforts into making things work, sometimes you just feel like you're not enough. Clearly, something is wrong if we all feel this way, whether we consciously accept it or not.

Pardon me for preaching, but the reasons for this are multiple; it could be the culture that we grew up in, which forced us to become perfectionistic and intolerant of failure. It could be trauma, where we lose our sense of safety, and we blame ourselves, as if we were the reason we were traumatized. It could be bullying, isolation, critical caretakers, neglectful parenting, or small errors that can cause self-image issues. Children being shamed earlier in life for their weight may go on to have crippling body image issues. I was bullied for my weight when I was little and then later in my teenage years, so that is something that stuck with me for a long time, and that I'm still conscious about.

For historic sociological (and genetic reasons), I don't know of (gracefully), we do live in a society that naturally leads to low self-esteem. We have great expectations that are set on everybody, regardless of whether they are humane or not. If your parents outright shame you for not achieving what they wanted, it becomes a real source of contention. You feel pressure to do better, but you also carry the weight of their judgements, and in time, that becomes suffocating; your brain learns to criticise yourself, and now that lives with you for good, the inner critic. You spiral, and maybe you could end up with an addiction later in life, which puts you in a feedback loop of self-denigration.

This is not to say that you should hate your caregivers; they are imperfect, flawed people who are products of their own circumstances. They may be just passing on what they received. So it is important to consider them with compassion as well. It doesn't absolve them of all faults, but we can be forgiving.

It is important to consider what dysfunctional patterns we have inherited from our caretakers. Has your parents' history become your own history? Are we living out the same pain that they have? How do we change it? These are some questions you may keep in mind for the next chapter.

When it comes to self-compassion, its application in this chapter is to handle new situations that come in and also heal the wounds of the past. Thankfully, they can both be approached in the same manner. So I'll be talking more about past wounds and unworthiness; leave it to you to extrapolate for newer pains.

After chapter one, we should have become a little more sensitive to what chatters inside of us. Try to look out for the voice of the inner critic, the censor

('The Artist's Way', Julia Cameron), which judges you perennially for what you did or did not do. "You did the reports wrong, you'll never be successful", "That drawing looks so pathetic, you're no artist", "She is bored with you and will leave you if you don't do something", "You can't read, how dumb are you?". If you haven't felt like this before, congratulations, you're lucky, or you need to really listen for it; maybe you've buried it with other things. This critical voice, whether you notice it or not, can be really grinding and wear you down. For me, I can recognize it as just a pang of anxiety, where I know I feel like I'm not good enough, that I have failed somehow, and I'm already scared of the censor before it has arrived. The inner critic is quite determined to keep you up and going. And from our non-judgmental exercises, the thing to recognize is that the inner critic is not good or bad, it is doing what it is doing, trying to keep us safe and protected, it tells us that if we do these things, we will be accepted and have physical, mental, and emotional safety. It is a survival skill that the inner critic runs on. So even if you feel really mad at this entity, try to look at it from this perspective, and don't resist it. These are a combination of the voices of people in your life. And remember, acceptance doesn't mean you give up; you just accept the chatter and move on.

As you may have guessed by now, an antidote to this particular problem is the quality of compassion.

Self-compassion has to do with treating yourself like you would treat a dear friend, or a child, maybe a baby. It is to recognize that we are suffering, and then to comfort and care and be kind to ourselves in that moment, holding ourselves in a space conducive to our needs. It is to be attuned to ourselves and to respond however we can. The first step of being compassionate is to know that we are suffering, which we have covered in the last chapter. Acceptance is to hold and possibly welcome the suffering. And then you tie it with some care in the form of words, actions, rituals, like sitting with yourself in front of a lit candle, being in silence. When your thoughts are striking and mean, bring in kindness and soft cushions, and let the tone of your voice when speaking to yourself be soft. Let's replace the tone of the inner critic with something kinder. Be it a current pain or a past pain, you deserve care. Self-compassion is about doing what's in your best interest, however. So, occasionally, you will have to push yourself to do something difficult, which is also love. For example, self-compassion doesn't mean you avoid the situations in front of you; it could mean that you tackle them head-on because that is what creates growth for you. Self-compassion doesn't mean that you wallow in self-pity, or drop your responsibilities, or push the blame onto other people, or blame a past self. It involves taking charge of your actions and understanding unpleasant truths. Maybe you have to do that scary thing. It's about accepting yourself and what you can do to help yourself, care for yourself, and nurture yourself. Be not afraid, says the six-winged fire eye.

Mimi purrs as if to encourage you to be okay with who you are, even if you're a little capybara in a big old world.

It may be that your inner critic and your sense of worthlessness may be so strong that it can deter you from trying to be caring with yourself, and wanting to avoid it. You might feel anger, "How dare she think she deserves happiness?", you might be ridiculed, "As if she could even". There is a deep amount of shame that you feel because of the inner critic, which can make you feel like the worst person. You must try to meet shame with self-compassion. If you feel tough resistance against being kind to yourself, just stick with the mindfulness, accept what your critic says, and tell yourself that you are here with yourself, that you are present with yourself, and that you are aware of your suffering. You don't have to be all lovey-dovey; it is enough to show that you are willing. It will feel easier over time, but for now, know that presence is a good start. I have a strong caregiver energy in me, but even then, I feel my critic so strongly that I don't want to take care of myself because I seemingly don't deserve it. So take your time with this; your body and mind have to adjust to the new truths that you find through acceptance and compassion. Like awareness, self-kindness is a muscle you have to train. And your sense of worth will turn around.

A few weeks into meeting my therapist, she told me something that changed my outlook on my worth. She told me that I've already gone through and survived the first big trauma that I've had, which is childbirth, to be separated from the mother and come into a strange world with sensory short-circuiting. You come into the world kicking and screaming, and you need love and soothing. It is your birthright to be deserving of love, happiness, and peace. I paraphrased a little extra, but it really gave me a sense of "Hey, I do belong, I do deserve love". That still sticks with me. Although I slipped back into self-loathing later several times, it's good to keep something like this in the back pocket. No one can tell you that you don't belong.

To start with self-compassion, let's take the acceptance exercise from the end of the last chapter and modify it. At this point, it is very much like RAIN(Tara Brach). The aim is to add kindness. So when you recognize and name your emotions, tell yourself that you see your emotions (either out loud, or silently in your head), that you will be present with your emotions, and your emotions are valid. You can decide on how you want to put it, but the idea is to show that we allow/welcome the emotion. Next, when you sit with the emotion, bring up some questions as if you are talking to the emotion like it is a person in need, questions like "What are you trying to tell me?" and "What do you need right now?". Try to be soft with the emotion, curious, not judgy, and just listen to what comes up; it might be words, imagery, or sounds. You may not understand at first what it means, but that's okay; the goal is to treat your inner systems with kindness. If you do get something, remember to provide it later, like playing a game of badminton, perhaps. You can end the exercise whenever you like. You should feel like a new dimension was added to your practice. Of course, being kind to yourself may not come to everybody, so just try to be as kind as you are willing to be. If the nervous system understands that there is some care in the system, it reacts differently. You can bring a sense of safety and certainty that you are a person who can take care of yourself.

It's good to go back to the exercises in chapter one and see where you can integrate bits of kindness into your practice. For instance, when you do a body scan, remind yourself that you are intentionally here to be with the body, that you are aware of the pain, and that you and this optimistic book are working together to ease your pain. The idea is that you can wield the power of your self-compassion in any tough situation.

You can practice being compassionate by sitting or standing in front of a mirror and talking to yourself. I find this exercise extremely difficult; you may not, but don't do this without help. When you talk to yourself like this, you may find that it is hard to be kind to yourself, and that's the point. We begin with just sitting with ourselves for five minutes, and eventually talking when you feel like it, and then slowly accepting who you are, physically, mentally, and emotionally. Emotions can come up like a volcano.

Over the course of the day, find a few minutes here and there and check in with yourself. "Hey, me, how are we feeling right now? Is there anything you need, like water? You did a good job washing the dishes. I appreciate having clean dinnerware…" It's about changing our inner dialogues. The more often we speak to ourselves this way, we change our narrative.

Self-Care Routine:

One of the aspects of self-compassion is to establish a self-care routine that addresses all your physical, mental, and emotional needs. It is literally a checklist of tasks to do to keep yourself content and at peace, such as getting enough sleep and hydrating. It may sound basic and trivial, but I find that it stabilizes my mood in surefire ways. I know for a fact that I can count on some of the tasks to lift my mood reliably. Although it can be taxing, maintaining regular care is extremely helpful and helps normalize your days (it evens out your mood). This is especially so when it comes to depression, where you tend to go offline and are unable to meet all your needs. Slowly working back up to a full routine is one part of overcoming your depression and restoring normalcy. It is about strengthening the trust you have in yourself that you can take care of yourself.

I'll be talking about different aspects of self-care that are ideally all naturally ticked off in a day. But don't be miffed if you can't do all of them, you can stick to 2-3 acts at first, any amount of self-care is good, it's more than none. Unfortunately, I don't have a neat mnemonic handy, so you'll just have to remember the aspects the old-fashioned way. They are all self-explanatory, so I won't get into detail, just suggest some tips.

Sleep. Everybody looks like they got socked following a night of disturbed or absent sleep. Our cognitive decline is very much apparent. It is pretty important to get some uninterrupted sleep and go through some REM cycles, deep sleep, and let dreams process the day for you, whether you remember them or not. Sleep is something I've had on-and-off problems with, and I know when it's going to be rough. It definitely makes depression worse and can reduce your tolerance for your emotions, anxiety, and general nonsense. It's also crucial for neuroplasticity so that we can learn new, healthier patterns to replace old, unhealthy ones.

Almost all the exercises from the last chapter are useful in bringing calm to the system, so you can use those to relax and drift off to sleep gently. You could go right from the middle of meditation into sleep. The mental phenomena exercise is good, just watching images come up in your brain and not really focusing on anything is supposedly similar to the hypnagogic state, where you transition into sleep. That helps me during afternoon naps, but not so much at night. It may work for you. Follow what blogs tell you; wind up with a book, or a story to tell yourself, dim all the lights, a short glass of milk, put on some white or brown noise or Brian Eno, avoid screens (I don't, to my own dismay), body scan, and just be in presence. If you have trouble, try something from the mental taxation section, math, categories in reverse alphabetical order, without much intensity, and slowly. It's just dull enough that you could drift off.

Exercise. I'm famously known for not being physical, but I have to say that I feel better every time after I exercise. It's just doing it that's the hard part. I love the first 10 seconds of running; it feels like I am channeling my ancestral heritage, and then I run out of breath and go home. But it feels like I can breathe better, my metabolism feels comfortable, my muscles all relax, my heart rate rests, and my mood just gets a lift. What's good for the gander of organs is good for the goose brain, or something. Of course, you don't need to do runs or heavy lifting; a brisk walk is good too, depending on whether you also want to work on being fit. A walk in nature is a very presence-oriented task that helps your physical and mental state. If you're sports-oriented, you can play some solo or group sports like squash or volleyball; there's the movement, plus the bonus of being around people. You get two in one, not bad. Try not to attach your self-esteem to how you played, though. Here we are just doing it to get the pipes working.

Now to address the problem of it being hard, borrowing from behavioral activation is a key thing; the process is one of the major ways in which you climb out of depression habits and/or procrastination. The idea I borrowed is that once you start a task, you will have momentum to continue it for some time, and the more often you can do it, the longer you will be able to go through with the task. You break it up into chunks. Let's say I need to work on my resume, but I can't get out of bed in the morning. What you could try is to split that process into smol tiny chunks; turn towards a side, sigh, sit up on the edge of the bed, stand, take a few steps, maybe go back to bed, or sit at your desk, open your laptop, sigh, move the cursor around, now you might as well check your resume, and now that we are here let's change the color of the heading. Now this is a little narrow, but it gives you the idea. You can set time limits, such as doing the dishes for two minutes, and that may be a small enough window that it feels possible. If you can just get the first step done, you will likely have some energy to continue. So even with exercise, start smol; maybe you do one push-up today, that's it, maybe you'll do two push-ups in three days. Some help is better than no help when you're suffering. It's important to recognize that you made the effort, however much it is; that's progress. Behavioral activation includes positive reinforcement by doing it with something that we enjoy, reengaging in the rewarding process. Editing that resume, even a bit, feels productive. You did it! But to start with, maybe it could be about drawing something, playing a video game.

Mimi rolls around trying to get up, but doesn't want to push herself up. When will our heroine have her snacks?

Nourishment. A well-balanced diet and frequent hydration are pillars of your well-being, or your body will show signs in time. Much of this you are already familiar with, I would imagine, so I'll just address my additions.

Cooking is a wonderful self-care activity; it shows that you care for yourself enough that you want to feed yourself. Not only that, it is a time for presence, self-trust, it is creative expression, and you can learn to make all sorts of dishes and change them up to your liking. It is nourishing for both the body and mind. It is also an excuse to go outside and buy groceries. It can be as easy as putting some rice and grams in a pressure cooker, or boiling an egg. The point is not to make dazzling dishes, but to give yourself something of your own to show that you are important, you are worth it.

It's also important to look out for the nourishment of the mind, and this is in what you do, who you surround yourself with, and what media you consume. Try to curate your scrolling and keep a mental timer on it; your brain starts short-circuiting after some point. For example, I curate my feed by manipulating the algorithm into showing me cute comics like Anna Laura or the beautiful works of False Knees, and that can still get grating; my brain feels heavy. Art, film, and music are all very subjective likings, so I can't recommend what will work for you. Choose to engage with something that keeps you afloat, affirming your values, giving you meaning, lifting your mood, and soothing your anxiety. It doesn't have to have a great cosmic meaning; just that it makes you laugh today, like the NLSS.

Connection. We are highly social creatures, and time with other people is important. We crave a sense of belonging and attachment, and want to make connections with other human beings, which can be facilitated through the most plain of conversation. Introverts and extroverts alike want and need connection, although the count varies. A lack of genuine connections in our lives leads to loneliness and isolation, and that is terrible for the mind, exacerbating any negative feelings and thoughts. Depression makes things worse. With how things are going with a lot of occupations, it can become really difficult to find time and energy during the week to connect with friends and family. Therefore, it's important to keep micro connections going, like sending a message about something that happened to you that day, or smiling at the cashier at the grocery store, or complimenting someone's outfit at the office. It may feel difficult because what if you don't get a response back? But more often than not, humans respond automatically to an attempt at genuine connection. Join Reddit communities or Discord servers, find forums, real-life pottery events, or something where you can meet like-minded people in real life. It could be while playing sports, at the gym, in a book club, at open mics, mental health groups. On the other extreme, if you can't live without people, try to find things that you can do alone, and ease yourself through the anxiety of being alone.

Some of us have wounds that are relational in nature; we were hurt in the context of a relationship, abuse, neglect, or betrayal, so we require healing that takes place through a relationship with your therapist or a compassionate mentor or friend, someone who will hold you without judgment. We need to find safety and trust in being in their company to help restore normalcy. Similarly, finding new connections helps us expand that feeling outward. Not everyone is going to be hurtful. You can protect yourself now, you've learnt to, and these small relationships can help you feel connected.

There is a quote that goes "The blood of the covenant is thicker than the water of the womb", which points out that you may form a chosen or found family that forms your closest knit relations instead of your actual family. And that is perfectly good. Some of us don't get the opportunity of living in a functional family, so we seek out people who fill in the roles of our spirit siblings. Bring in people who align with your values. Let them be Saturday movie night people and Sunday cry time people.

Mimi wants you to be compassionate with yourself when you're swimming through dating apps. It's a lot. We need Mimi the Matchmaker!

When it comes to romantic relationships, one pattern that I want to bring up that I have learned to deal with, the hard way, is codependency, for either party. It kind of shows you that self-compassion takes a more protective and tough route. Typically, in a codependent relationship, there is one who provides and the other relies to the point that their relationship is predicated on that dynamic. It can show up in different ways depending on attachment styles; how you relate to a person is based on how you're raised. For example, it might be that one person is cold and distant and doesn't communicate directly, or hides on purpose, pushes people away, just out of fear and prejudgment, whereas the other is compensating for every mood shift and is afraid that person will leave and not have anyone to care for them. The caretaker may try to control the other and manipulate them in subtle ways to stay. They most often end up shutting down their own needs and mask and lie so the relationship stays stable. They efface themselves for the other out of fear. It can also be that both parties take turns in these roles. These are not compassionate ways of being in the relationship for either person.

What you want to do instead is to set healthier communication patterns between you two and also have strong boundaries in place. Both of you need to take space and put a limit on how you spend yourself or rely on the other person. All relationships involve dependency, but the idea is that you do not get lost in the other; you have to remind yourself that you are a person independent of the other. You have a life of your own as well to live.

And that's big compassion. Begin to trust each other by talking about how you really feel, and get counseling help if you think you need someone to help you mediate and suggest actions. This isn't an invitation to stop being caring; this is to ensure that neither party is overwhelmed by the relationship.

I ended up being a deep caregiver for somebody; I was really enmeshed with this person, where my whole life wanted to revolve around them. I was cognizant of it, but could not detach. Things forcibly ended later, and it left a gulch where the person used to be. I'm still healing from that wound.

Anyway, not trying to scare you out of a relationship. Just a friendly nudge to read up about healthy relationship patterns like listening, understanding, trusting, and safety. It's not a "me vs you" affair, but "us v-s the problem", teamwork. You want to build a solid foundation for the future where both people are nurturing the relationship, and it is a work-in-progress. You want to build habits where you co-regulate with each other, maybe do some parallel play in the same room, like drawing, painting, gaming, reading, but separately. It really does help you feel closer.

Having pets can be helpful for company, although it takes a long think to determine whether you can take care of yourself and a pet. Don't go in unless you know you can handle it; otherwise, the responsibility may bring stress.

Mimi isn't a pet, she's an important guide. That being said, scratches are welcome. And so are coupons for organic tea powder.

If you have a spiritual leaning, make time in your day to spend a few minutes connecting with your higher self/wiser self/oversoul, in whatever form that you want to view it. Maybe burn some incense, sit down in front of an object of your choice, and just pray for what your heart longs for in the moment, maybe human connections. Ritual has a way of making the intangible tangible, and the expression of your thoughts and feelings are ways that work well to process them. More on that in a later chapter.

Play. There is a part of us that wants to play with others and ourselves, the innocent child part of us that wants to enjoy things for the sake of it, not to aim for goals and achievements, but to just tinker around and explore in the sandbox. They say that the older you get, the larger your toys get. Of course, you don't need to have monster trucks to have fun, although I haven't experienced one yet, so I can't say. But we can manage with what is probably much easier to source. Playing activities include drawing and doodling Pokémon, singing and playing a ukulele, dancing around to classical music, playing with Legos or Minecraft, or reading a story, maybe a comic, and Dark Souls. All these activities are designed to be open-ended; the point is to just let yourself play. We're going to dedicate a smol chapter on this towards the end.

Finally, the last two I have to mention, but don't have too much to talk about, are **grooming** and **gratitude.**

Brush your teeth, wash your face, take a bath however you can, and dress yourself up in something you like, style your hair, even if you're not going outside, there is something to it that makes grooming a charging mechanism. I find that if I do get that far, then doing the other tasks also becomes easier; it's behavioral activation. And it can make you feel good about how you look, and fragrant smells, that's a mood booster. Plus, not to mention just having good hygiene in general.

Gratitude is something I have a lot of difficulty with, but if I'm in a place to be able to feel it, it makes everything else seem wonderful and easy. You don't have to feel thankful for you to practice gratitude; you just need to think thankfully for that one thing that helped you. It is another muscle that needs to be trained. You could get a jar, and every night you could write what you're thankful for on a piece of paper and put it in the jar. Later, you can empty it and read all the things that made you feel that way, and that enriches your experiences. It can even help to be grateful for things you haven't experienced yet, like being thankful for a class going well, and that helps with how you go about doing it.

Mimi is happy to have you around; she's thankful you've been sincerely following along. She gives you an orange flower. But then she wants it back for lunch.

Wait, there's one more thing I'm missing out on, oops. One of the strongest factors for being resilient through difficulty is having a good sense of **humour.** If you can laugh yourself out of pain, that's a good quality to have. It doesn't mean burying your pain again and avoiding it, but to be able to see the light in the situation. To laugh in this way, with the pain, is to accept things. We open our hearts to what is happening to us, around us. Be silly, spend time around people who make you laugh, notice the absurdity of human living, and watch some comedy specials. Cultivate a humor you can wield.

And that concludes our section on self-care. Hopefully, you have some plans on how to incorporate some of the exercises into your week; your mind-body complex will thank you for it. Shifting to self-compassion is real change work; you'll find yourself appreciating it when you do it without realizing it. That's one way to know that your practice is really sinking in.

Compassion externally:

Self-compassion isn't complete without understanding the other, as we don't exist in a vacuum. All of us are interlinked in some large graph network, and our actions determine the well-being of ourselves as well as others. The more we bring our peaceful selves to the show, the more we spread peace to other people. If you show that you care, people tend to care back. The more you practice one (self or external), the easier it is to execute the other.

We are all linked by our common humanity; we are going through hard journeys that take many different forms, but ask for the same basic thing: love. We are not alone in our hardship, and sometimes that is a good anchor. Just like it takes a village to raise a child, the adult needs the village just as much as the village needs the adult. I hope what I am saying makes sense to you. It is the Buddha's compassion towards others that made him go looking for the root of dukkha (suffering) and transcend it. He could've done sick kick flips in Nirvana, but stayed on earth to teach everyone else what he learnt. So your self-compassion work matters not just to you, but to your community as well. It is both meaning and compassion that egged me on to write this book, so I could help ease suffering in my own way.

I'm borrowing from Kristin Neff here, as her tenets are mindfulness, kindness, and connectedness; they are central to self-compassion. We've already touched upon the first two in this book, so I figure I should add a section on connectedness as well.

When interacting with others, one of the most rewarding connecting skills to have is the quality of **listening.** The act is very simple, but it can be difficult given our own impaired attention because of flash media and self-centeredness, even if you don't mean to. It's something that's not hard to fix. To listen is to give them your rapt attention, which is something you've gained from the first chapter, and take in what people are sharing with you earnestly. If they're talking about pumpkins, just try and listen to every word they say and be present. You might notice that you have genuine questions about pumpkins that you want to ask. Active listening involves paying attention to the nonverbal cues, too, like silences and changing voices. It involves reflecting what they say back to them, soft affirmations to indicate you heard something, and asking questions. It is a wonderful way to keep conversations going.

Listening is another task, like cooking, that blends presence and compassion. Listen to people like how you want to be heard. People love people who listen; they enjoy the presence you bring into their lives. You also learn a lot about the other person.

On a side note, this skill may be useful for you to grow your empathy as you learn how the other person feels, through listening. For those of you who may have empathy circuits wired wonky, at least this may help you understand what the other person is thinking and what their stance may be.

For both external and internal compassion, there is a practice called loving kindness meditation (**metta).** This is a nice way to reorient how we feel about ourselves and others through regular practice. The goal is to extend our compassion starting from ourselves, to someone you love, to someone you feel neutral about, and to someone you have trouble with. Repeat to yourself some statement that offers compassion, for example, "May you/I be kind to yourself/myself, may you/I be loved, may you/I find peace". You may change the order according to what you have difficulty with. If you find it harder to love yourself, place yourself last. The exercise trains your kindness muscle as if you're going up weight classes, and opens your heart to all kinds of people. It is quite a drastic change to wish peace on a person who has hurt you in the past, but if you can, you've really become a student of compassion.

Of course, it is really important in compassion work to have **boundaries**, without which we would just turn into a puddle of everyone's suffering. Being compassionate to others does not mean that we let ourselves be harmed, drained, and shaken. It is an act of self-compassion to enforce boundaries, to protect yourself, as well as letting the other stand on their own two feet. Being a wounded healer, it is very difficult for me to say no to someone who is suffering, with or without meaning to. But it is essential you do not take on their burdens, as that weight will only burden you. It doesn't mean you are abandoning them; it just means you have to take care of yourself presently. Make it clear how much you can do. Like Virgil says to Dante in DmC3, "If you cannot protect yourself, then who else can you protect?" You need energy to sustain your compassionate efforts; sometimes you just have to kindly offer a no. And it wasn't clear to me, but you don't need to suffer to understand somebody else's suffering, you don't need to suffer to help others, that is something some of us who have enmeshed ourselves with somebody else's mind may not realize. Protect your mind. My therapist once drew multiple concentric circles and told me I could keep friends in one circle, family in another, but the innermost is only for yourself, not to be misshapen by another.

Mimi says no when the monkeys ask too much of her for playtime. They are sad, but they respect Mimi for her forthrightness. She doesn't want to be in the chaos.

And the last thing I would like to mention about compassion is the concept of **forgiveness**. This is quite a difficult topic to talk about for many of us, and is something that took me a very long time before I could truly accept it. You can forgive other people, and you can forgive yourself; both are important and a part of being compassionate. What helped me see it humanely was reading the book on forgiveness by Desmond Tutu, where he talks about the Truth and Reconciliation Mission. There are stories in there of people who have murdered others during the apartheid era in South Africa, and it tells of their release by families who were affected by their actions. They confessed the damage they caused, talked about the story of the violence they committed, and had a chance to ask for forgiveness. Surprisingly, many of them were forgiven by the affected families after hearing their story. Then they had a choice of releasing or renewing their relationship, and some ended up staying as gardeners with those families. Quite a strange change. Compassion is like that, a surprising change. Forgiveness does not condone the violence, and it does not stop justice, but it can release the pain from both parties.

Perhaps try employing the four steps in your own life: recognize that you have made a mistake, tell yourself the story, ask yourself for forgiveness, and try granting it, and renew your relationship with yourself. It is okay if it does not come naturally; give it time. You may feel deeply ashamed by what you did, but treat yourself as a human. What forgiveness does is that it takes away the pain, that resentment, and that anger at you or the other, all of which is harmful to your system. Be big enough to accept that you've made an error, that you willingly or unwillingly hurt somebody. You're not any smaller for it. The admission precedes healing.

Inner Child Work:

There is one modality that I would like to introduce at this point, now, instead of a later chapter. Like I had mentioned earlier, a lot of our wounds come from childhood events, how we were treated by our caretakers, as well as other people, other children. Inner child work posits that there is a part of us that is a child, innocent, playful, but may be hurt and dysfunctional. We are used to hearing people say "A part of me wants …", so similarly, there's a part of you that is still a child and wants childlike things. Therapy with the inner child involves talking internally to that child, having dialogue that is supportive and validating, and a means to try and meet the unmet needs of your inner child, things like affection, safety, emotional regulation, and structure. So you would sit there in a quiet place, be in presence, and go something like "Hey kiddo, I'm here to see you. What would you like to do today?", and listen for what comes up. A helpful tip is that it should just come up naturally; you don't have to force a response. An image or message will come. We talk to the child compassionately and reinforce safety in the child, "Don't worry, I'm going to be here when you need me". You can include the child in all your adventures throughout this book if you feel inclined to do so. If you're meditating in presence, imagine that your child is also sitting quietly with you. When you do art, imagine you are painting what she wants you to see. Go out on play-dates for your child. I added this here because taking care of a child is a thing of compassion; it may help many of you connect closer to yourself through this framework. Remember, if you can't be compassionate, just offer presence for now. "I am here."

Consider reading a summary of Stefanie Stahl's "The Child In You", and see if you would like to give it a full read. It's a well-cooked piece of work, capturing just the right details such that it all makes sense. A large part of the book is to learn about what protection strategies our inner child employs to meet our basic needs(connection, autonomy, pleasure, acknowledgement), like avoidance, wanting control, masking/lying, aggression, and what to replace them with. For example, my scared inner child tends to employ masking and lying to seek acknowledgement; he wants to be seen in a semi-positive light. Instead, we could try being authentic and provide my inner child with validation internally. The book is about healing your hurt child and embodying the sun child, which is a confident, peaceful, curious, optimistic, sunny version.

Interesting fact: when trauma happens, where you couldn't process or overcome the event, it gets stored in the limbic system of your brain, and the memory is stuck at the age at which it happened. So, quite literally, our connections are in childhood, which assigns some physical component to the inner child. Overcoming the trauma means reworking the limbic system. Cool to see a physical component linked to the modality.

So we have reached the end of the second chapter. You have the tools you need to live a peaceful life, and you have the heart of Siddhartha. As always, practice makes almost perfect. We don't need to be perfect, but we sure could try for it.

Be kind.

Mimi leads you through the bushes into the Temple of Aquarius. There are several worn-out travellers leaning against the broken structures. They have built a sort of community here where help remains a constant, no matter who comes and goes. You and Mimi also take rest and massage your feet gently; that was a long walk. You share your oranges with a group of parrots that are gossiping beside you. Mimi grunts to indicate not to give away too many oranges; they are hers. The statue of Lady Aquarius gazes lovingly at you. You feel the warmth of your own heart responding back.

✦✦✦

CHAPTER 3

CLARITY

This chapter is going to briefly cover digging into our minds and examining our thoughts and feelings about ourselves and the world, and possibly amend them to what may be helpful for you. You may feel like being a detective, Sherlock Go Holmes. We learned how to hold our mental phenomena in the first two chapters, but now is the time to understand more about them. To think of a metaphor for this chapter, on my walk to work, there's one loose tile on the sidewalk that juts upward slightly that I, and others, have tripped over multiple times. This work is to identify and measure the tile, remove and replace it with a newer tile, making the path smooth. Wish someone would do that for the actual tile. What is the tile? Your thoughts.

The things I am going to be talking about are from my own experiences with CBT, so this isn't a clinically correct guide to it, but just notes on how you can employ thinking to understand yourself better. I got a sort of crash course from my therapist through practice, and it worked for me, so hopefully it will help you too.

We briefly mentioned in the first chapter about writing down our thoughts as we encounter them during meditation. Those thoughts will be useful now. But don't worry, we can sit and access our thoughts again now. Just recall the meditation on mental phenomena, and you can use that as an exercise to find out what is on your mind today and examine that.

So the premise behind the work we are going to do is that thoughts (what your brain says), feelings (what your body says), and behavior are connected together in the form of a triangle; thoughts lead to feelings, feelings lead to behaviors, behaviors result in reinforcing the thought (negative or positive). For example, I think that I made a big mistake today. I feel empty and in pain, because of the pain, I get drunk, and then I think about what a bad mistake this was, and that loops, reinforcing my idea that I'm broken or something. Another one is that you think of going over to make friends with someone, but you suddenly think you're too dumb, then you feel ashamed and anxious, and you don't go make friends, and that brings you to think you're too stupid and a coward. "I could never make friends". There are many examples that you could overlay over this framework.

If our mind behaves in this way, then what people suggest is that if we mess with any of the three, then it'll have an impact on the other two, and may change how the situation goes on. For example, if we hold our pain compassionately (change our feeling), then maybe we could expose ourselves to something we're anxious about instead of avoiding it (our behavior), and that makes our thoughts go "I did it! I beat Gael the Slave Knight" and positively reinforce ourselves for next time. Although it may seem simplified, it works well in practice, and what you can benefit from is that you can identify problems in your life and apply this framework to see if you can make a change (most likely).

So what we have to do is pay attention to our **automatic thoughts**; they just happen off the cuff as a reaction to something. Thanks to the evolutionary negativity bias we have in us, we are more likely to notice the negative rather than the positive, or the neutral. That means a lot of the time, we have these automatic negative thoughts (ANTs, cute) that are going on and on around things outside and inside of us. Some examples include thoughts and beliefs like "He's not paying attention to me, so that must mean he doesn't like me," or "Why bother trying? I'll fail anyway," or "If I get sick, the department will fall apart", or "It's all my fault my parents got divorced". The thoughts come out as reactions due to some past pain experienced, probably in childhood, and they really make things difficult for us. It's like being unable to walk properly; your negative thoughts weigh you down.

Now, negative thoughts aren't bad; they are messengers, saying that something feels off. Shame could've meant survival to our ancestors. But if it repeats over time and becomes a nasty pattern, they become beliefs like "I'm not good enough", and make our lives harder. Instead of doing things, we hide behind our beliefs, and you don't need to hide; you're perfectly capable of living a healthier life. We just have to do a bit of work to address these patterns and replace them with healthier thoughts.

Mimi used to think a lot about her weight. But then she realized she is the largest rodent in the world. Talk about a flex.

Identifying these antsy thoughts can be a little tricky. One way is to think of places you had trouble in your life in recent times, where you were sad, anxious, overwhelmed, angry, and ask yourself what was happening inside your head. Try to relive that experience you've had (not something traumatic right away) and figure out what thoughts you had before or after you were sad. For example, when you were in the cafeteria, you saw a classmate walk by who is really smart, and you felt sad.

What were your thoughts? Maybe it was like "Oh, I can't ever be like them", that is an ANT to pick up, maybe there were more thoughts after, like "I'm too undisciplined to get into university". The first part may be true, but the conclusion is a negative belief. Another way to notice ANTs is the mental phenomena meditation, seeing what thoughts come up naturally about yourself, others, and the world in general. An exercise that I did was to take a notebook and give myself the prompt "I believe I am..." or "I believe others are...", or "I think the world is..." and then just kept writing whatever came into my mind, whether it made sense or not. Do this for 5-10 minutes. Later, I reviewed it and picked out the negative beliefs, such as "I am broken". When you first start doing this, try to track your thoughts in the notebook; you can come back and work on some later. You'll begin to see a lot of places that could use compassion.

Now, these negative beliefs often end up showing you a distorted view of yourself and the world, they klishta your perception and you derail. For example, thinking that you can't go to university in the earlier example could be an error in how you view yourself. Maybe you are minimizing yourself and underestimating your ability to get into a prestigious program. Instead, you perceive yourself as unable and not rigorous enough, even though that may be far from the truth. Your view of yourself is preventing you from reaching your actual potential, and that is why it's important to understand it and change it. So, like this particular error, there are multiple common **distortions** or errors that can tell you what your belief clouds are. It may help you understand how the belief is affecting you. I'll quickly touch upon each one with an example or two. See which ones you identify with your thoughts.

Cognitive distortions:

- All-or-nothing/Black-or-white thinking, thinking in extremes
  - "If I'm not liked by everyone, I must be worthless",
  - "This has to be perfect or I'm a failure."
- Magnification/minimization, either making things bigger or smaller than they are.
  - "Oh, I said the word wrong, everyone's going to think I'm stupid."
- Mind reading, trying to predict what someone is thinking.
  - "Oh, my professor didn't talk to me cause I messed up."
- Fortune telling, trying to predict how events will transpire.
  - "This presentation is going to be so bad, i know it."

- Jumping the gun, making a quick conclusion with no evidence.
  - "He didn't give me a voucher; it must be because he doesn't like me."
- Personalization, centering yourself as the reason why things happen.
  - "Oh, it's my fault that we got attacked."
- Overgeneralization, making a general statement based on a specific event.
  - "Everything is ruined because of this candle."
- Catastrophizing, thinking that the worst things possible will happen.
  - "The interview is going to bomb."
- Mental filtering, taking in only the negative.
  - "Those two people didn't seem interested in my drama; it must not be very good."
- Discounting the positive, excluding or minimizing the positive.
  - "I only passed the test by luck."
- Emotional reasoning, making logical statements based on how you feel.
  - "I don't get a good feeling from her; she must be horrible."

- Should/must statements.
    - "I must always be calm/loving"

You don't have to memorize this; you'll soon get used to the feel of these ways of thinking and be able to pick up on them in your day-to-day, especially if you relate to them. On a side note, sometimes your intuition may be right when it comes to thinking about something; your mind-reading of your spouse might be accurate. That's an evolutionary ability we have, to understand emotion from body language and behaviors. But in general, it is better to act when evidence is available and not make assumptions and wrong conclusions. I say this to point out that our gut brain does have quick inferencing skills and is useful, but take the time and examine your thoughts and reality to see if they make sense. Be critical here, not to yourself.

"?!" says Mimi every time you make a cognitive distortion. Wherever did you get that idea, my love?

Now that we have learned to pick out these thoughts and have understood that they color our perception of the world, what can we do about these negative thoughts? You can treat these thoughts with compassion "Oh I'm sorry that you feel like you're too much" and then sit with the emotion, and maybe from that place you will say "You know you're not too much right? You weren't out of line." or something soothing knowing that whatever you did was not a big deal. Maybe for "I won't ever be like them", you respond with "Maybe not, but I'm certainly capable". "He must hate me" can turn into "Oh, he's just busy with work". This particular process is called **reframing**, and it's about changing your negative thoughts to a positive or neutral one that fits your circumstances. Instead of the negative thought, you replace it with something helpful and true, which changes your perception about yourself and the world, giving you forward momentum to tackle your difficulties. Over time, they give you a sense of confidence and optimism. It takes practice to reframe your thoughts, and it needs time to settle into your system. Once it does, you'll find yourself automatically examining and spinning thoughts in helpful ways.

It is important to identify which parts of your thoughts aren't the full truth. Like that statement about being undisciplined might be true for that person, but saying you won't get into university is a belief. They could reframe it as "I am not so rigorous, but I'm smart enough to catch up on things," or "I will commit a little more time to getting things done," or "I'm not good at math, but maybe I can ask someone to help me". The new replacement thought is subjective to your life, so you need to figure out what a helpful thought would be, which are the solutions to your problem.

We've focused on thoughts that mostly involve a negative perception of yourself, but you may have thoughts that focus on other people or society, or the world in general, "Like my parents are to blame for my situation," or "Society is stopping me from living free". Please examine these thoroughly as well, because they may be true, but you can find helpful reframes that are focused on your own agency. These are thoughts that come from the environment you grew up in.

Typically, examining these thoughts is done in dialogues between you and your therapist, but you can engage in a dialogue with yourself, maybe even write it down as it happens. We learn to question our thoughts critically to know more about them, to see if they are true, and to come up with ways to move ahead. In therapy, you do it through a process called **Socratic Dialogue.** My therapist calls it verbal challenging and tells me to fight like dirty lawyers. Anyway, Socrates is said to have taught his students by deeply questioning their understanding of things. Like if somebody said "Oranges are healing", you could follow up with "How do you know oranges are healing?", and the student would have to substantiate their claim. Was it just something he heard, or was there evidence he knew? Then another question would follow, perhaps about one who gave him this information.

Socrates was known to be quite cutting, but we can be a little softer, unless you're into it.

The first thing you want to do is pick up the belief you want to work on. Perhaps meditate and do some exercises from chapter one so that you can be in presence and less clouded, open, patient, and non-judgmental. Ask some questions to try and clarify the question, what makes you feel this way, when and where it has come up, how you address it, and who you were with. The 5Ws and H help elicit responses. You can practice digging into things by choosing things like "I like Pacific Rim" and asking why you like it, and questioning your responses to get to the most basic ideas of why you like it.

Mimi pulls up on a horse. It's time to follow the thought train, like we're stealing gold.

Let's say we got a thought "I'm too nervous, I am incompetent for band", here you could ask questions about the incompetence part, what makes you think you are, i.e., what evidence is there that you are incompetent, and also ask what evidence there is that you are competent. Your identification of cognitive distortions will help you question any follies, and you can challenge that knowing it's wrong. From there, you can ask a compassionate question like "What would you say if your friend said this?" and see if you respond with something lighter.

You can point out any double standards that you're perpetuating. You could also ask, "What would Jeremy in band class tell me if he spoke?" What's an alternative perspective? When you feel it, ask yourself what it would be to drop the negative belief? Would you feel better? Accordingly, think about reframing belief with something more compassionate, realistic, and whole - "I play decently enough to be in band class, and I'm capable of learning more".

This is a short, direct example where I asked for evidence right out of the gate without digging, but you could go deeper. If you question the incompetence, maybe it comes out that your parents made you feel dumb when you were a child, maybe less than a sibling. It's a good moment to help yourself with presence and kindness, now you know that you are capable, "Oh, Daddy and Mommy weren't so nice when you were small, but look at you now, you've developed into a wonderful human creature and you've done so many things like....".

Another one could be that you are angry at your husband for being cold about something you love. You might have to go looking for why you feel cold, who else made you feel this way, maybe you had coworkers who treated you poorly for a long time, who were cold to your ideas. And see if you can separate out that your husband is not like your coworkers, and/or you can work on this in therapy. It might get a little tense, but you know how to defuse.

Anyway, in short, elicit and clarify the belief with questions, start to challenge the belief, and/or look for alternate views, be compassionate, and then start reframing and problem-solving to figure out what concrete steps, small or not, that you can take to stop this belief from continuing to persist.

A word of caution is that you don't want to spend a lot of time thinking, and thinking, because that just starts to be rumination and that's another problem to deal with. Set a timer for how long you would like to think and stick to it, maybe 15 minutes or 45 if deep. It will get quicker once you start becoming more aware of your inner ecosystem. Your brain will be able to pick out why or what very quickly. Some of you may have especially clever brains and try to build complex structures, and say that you can't do anything because of this and that. Take a step back and try to figure out what you want to avoid or love, and go there and see what small steps you can take. The whole thing will crumble based on one small belief you thwart. Also, insight doesn't heal you; integration does. You can sit at home and figure out all your beliefs, but you have to go out there and do practical things based on your insight, embody practices, and dance around in a fountain. The nervous system needs to be tuned, too.

The last thing I would like to mention is the importance of having a **value system**. A value system is simply how you feel about different kinds of values, like honesty and creativity and curiosity, and bravery; it is your feelings on what values are important to you in your life. You may not have consciously thought that "Oh, I want this value and that value", but you have a value system that you adopted through your formative years. An exercise you can do is to get a whole bunch of values from Google or ChatGPT or whatever else, and put a rating out of 5 or 10 that tells you how much you align with having that value. Keep track of which ones are the most important. The task then is to start thinking about your life in terms of these values and how closely you are living your life according to the values that you do like. If it doesn't align, try a dialogue and see where it gets you. The idea is that these values can now act as guiding lights when it comes to decision-making. You want to be authentic. You want to make choices that are in line with what you chose, as that will give you strength and meaning. It is a simple and short idea, but it could have long-term consequences in how you live your life. Your values may also change in time depending on what experiences you have, so don't sweat it if that happens.

I typically don't remember to do this, but I remind myself now and again what it feels like to live with curiosity. That is an important value I hold; everything that I enjoy, including this writing, comes from a question of either curiosity or compassion. Be adventurous, be kind, be inquisitive, and be gentle.

And that's the end of this chapter. I have a habit of overthinking and not executing, so this is one of my weaker chapters when it comes to my own path. I hope this was helpful for you and you've learned a new way to talk with your thoughts and assumptions, and beliefs. May your wise mind show you truths.

Be clear.

Spending time in the Archival Cathedral was more rewarding than expected. Mimi took you to the shelves that had been stacked with your own thoughts since birth; the Great Archivist had taken it all down and made notes. Mimi curled underneath a desk, tired, while you went through the books and paid attention to where the Archivist made gentle observations and summaries of your mind. It gives you clarity about your endless spout of thoughts, all non-judgmentally, unprovoked. The church/library is quiet and cool, except for the occasional shuffling in the distance. You could nod off.

✦✦✦

CHAPTER 4

EXPRESSION

In this chapter, we're going to take a deeper look into putting our thoughts and feelings from being these fuzzball things inside of us to fully formed writing, art, music, and whatever ways to express. This chapter is an invitation to invoke the creative in you, to build worlds and characters and immerse in your theatre, imaginary yet so dramatic and realer than real, singing songs of the earth, painting the dreamy backdrop. This is all about building a relationship with art and play and recognizing wholeness. Keep an open mind to these concepts even if you have some nasty associations with drawing or writing. Immerse yourself through presence and compassion to move past any icks. We're not looking to make the next Undertale, just mess around.

Mindfulness keeps you grounded, self-compassion turns kindness inwards, and structured thinking gives a way to reengineer our beliefs. So, what does creative expression give us? There are different reasons as to why we engage with art for healing in this book; one is that it cultivates a free and open space where you can express your mind and play around with things. When we're stuffed up with our lives, having an outlet to just be open, honest, real, flowing, and creatively engaged can be a lifesaver. It is important in the context of this chapter to not view art as something to achieve; that can come later. Be curious, we're exploring what we can make. The times when I have written lots of music were when I was open to ideas and going down rabbit holes. The thrill of just listening to your wonky ideas played back is amazing.

Second, you can use it as a means of getting your thoughts and feelings onto something outside you, the transfer of material to something tangible, formless to form. Expression of your inner world may not always come through verbally. It could be a picture that you drew of something inside you that leads to insight. My therapist uses art therapy to figure out what's going on in my unconscious mind about a topic. We sit and discuss different things I've drawn, the colours that I've used, and what I can learn from them. It's about insights as well as emotional release through working with personal symbols.

Thirdly, it is a means of connecting with almost universal human experiences; you may hear music that helps describe how deeply lonely you feel, and this music may connect you to other like-minded people, or you might write a song that resonates with hundreds about your experience. It allows for your unique perspective to be seen by others. In early human history, art was used to communicate with others, pass down beliefs, and as part of rituals. It brought the community together. It still brings people together. Your art is a way for you to be seen in a way that you otherwise wouldn't be.

Fourthly, art can be a way of making meaning. It gives you something to work towards, perhaps leaving a legacy, or just cultivating a creative life, maybe a rebellion against forced normality. Maybe it becomes a means to rewrite your own story, change the narrative of your life into one of agency, into something dear to you. Finding more about yourself, making your unconscious known, and finding wholeness is the center of art-based inner work. You will discover things about your current problems, but will also find deeper healing, maybe of generational wounds, even.

You could get started with the exercises I'll give you at any time. It may be just about engaging with a bunch of Legos or Play-Doh. The only advice you need is to not let anything stop you. Find some private time and space to let your system say what it wants to say, even if it's only ten minutes of creative output. The practice may not feel very open and playful at first, especially if you have a nasty inner critic, but keep a lookout for moments that do capture that energy, a non-judgmental mind, and invite the next action. Over time, these sessions will become more engaging. Don't stop at the slightest sense of discomfort. This is good training to build resistance against that. Don't turn fun into a goal; let it just be like you're a monkey who hasn't seen a piano before. Offer a banana, snack time, and play time. I don't even know why monkeys and bananas are so associated.

We've already covered presence, so that will be our entry point into and during the exercises. Be compassionate towards yourself when you draw, whether you're scared, or feel like you're going to do a bad job, or you feel like it is pointless. Hold yourself up through the process; there is nothing to lose. We will apply our critical thinking skills from the last chapter, but for the start of the exercises, it is just doing, mostly with no guiding light other than your own.

A thing that is useful to know is that we employ a lot of what is called **symbolism**, which prevails throughout a lot of artwork. Things are rarely what they seem to be, and truth is subjective. A symbol is an object that represents some kind of concept, usually abstract and intangible, like love, charm, or misery. For example, one may paint a dog into a picture to represent the quality of loyalty and obedience, or maybe if it's a stray, it represents not having a home, or maybe it is about having freedom, or maybe you had a dog that ran away that you're concerned about. Each person can assign personal meanings to a symbol they interact with. Carl Jung talks about there being signs, which have one general meaning, like a stop sign, and symbols as having meaning beyond the obvious signage. A symbol is deep and has hidden meanings we may not know of, ever. In this sense, the dog is a symbol to the viewer and the artist, as each has a different significance to attribute. Although the artist chooses meaning ahead of time sometimes, it could still evoke other things for him. Symbols can also have a collective nature from universal aspects like the Mother or Father, so sometimes symbols may additionally have this meaning too. They're referred to as archetypes and symbols that come from these unconscious patterns. Like cows are seen as very motherly, that image might be coming from the Mother pattern. A broken home could mean exactly that. To me, it feels like almost anything can be a symbol if you can find personal meaning, some resonance, but I ain't no Jungian analyst. Art can be a bridge between the conscious and unconscious mind, and Jung believed our unconscious talks to us through the language of symbols. We can't help but go that deep, because studying what our art means to us is a means to understanding what plays out inside of us, like in dreams.

Mimi wonders what she symbolizes to you. What kind of figure do you see her as? Is there sass?

When we do our exercises, I will sometimes ask you to do something without thinking, for example, put colors in without thinking, but feel. So what I ask of you is that I want you to draw from the unconscious, and not the conscious mind. You have agency over the conscious mind; you can choose to draw a duck. But to draw from the unconscious, you have to listen to what the unconscious is saying. This is where that listening skill from chapter two gets in handy. Just keep an open mind and wait for images or language, colors, and sounds. You'll know it is from the unconscious if it comes spontaneously, although it may transform. It is like watching the surface of a pond, and bubbles of air pop out; you do not force the bubbles, they just appear. If you've practiced the mental phenomena meditation, then this will make more sense to you. So, when I ask you to draw without thought, this is what I mean.

This is a section of the book that gets into some woo-woo, but don't let that turn you away. Your conversation with your art reveals things because it is about your honest thoughts and feelings that come up as a response to what is created. The art acts as a mirror in which you see yourself. This may have come out with talk therapy, but like I mentioned earlier, art helps bring out nonverbal information in the brain, and it provides distance from your problems, emotionally regulates them, and lets you process them. There are multiple brain regions activating, and the brain is relearning what it experienced in past memories.

You can do these exercises with a trusted friend, with both of you involved in parallel play. It helps you co-regulate, and your interpretations may help the other find meaning from their art through elimination. The only warning is not to get caught up in the other completely; the art has personal significance to you first.

Instead of calling them exercises, you can also think of exercises being **rituals** of some kind; they are symbolic acts taken for some particular purpose, and they give a sense of sacredness to your work. So if you are drawing about your partner who left you, the symbolic act of it may be to gain peace from that incident, you can float down your art paper in a stream to invoke releasing that relationship, and weirdly, the brain accepts that as processing your wound. I've heard in a few different places that your brain doesn't differentiate symbols from the object, dreams from reality. Whether it is true or not, it is helpful for us to try it out, with nothing to lose.

Mimi walks around in a few circles around a few oranges. It's a thankfulness ritual before she takes them for bathing.

Now, one last thing before we get into the doing, which is a paragraph on my own experiences with play and art therapy. It may give you some understanding of how it could be for you.

When I met my therapist back in 2023, it was immediately back-to-back sessions in what was called sand play therapy, which was developed in the 1950s as a means of helping children communicate how they feel to the therapist through toys in the sand. Their actions give way to what's on their mind. There was once when I picked up a few plastic insects and placed them in water with a baby in the center. Unintentionally, I had picked up a beetle, which is a symbol somewhere for father, and a moth, which is mother. And the moth sank down, like it was repressed. The baby just floated with no help. My therapist told me all this later. I had sort of given away my dysfunctional family. Similarly, I had once unconsciously drawn the outline of a foetus in the sand. These all spoke of developmental impediments being in a childlike state. Simultaneously, on those days I was also painting, and that uncovered different things; a red swan in the distance as if watching, a dark household, and that pointed to my own disconnection with my feelings and suppressed aggression, and a lack of stability. It became a means of talking about my inner world, and then we did troubleshooting using talk therapy or CBT. I had to develop into an adult from a fearful, unsure, child-like state, and that required facing things, which was difficult, but could've been easier through our first two chapters. Anyway, I hope you got a feel for how play and art can bring out different thoughts and feelings. You could discover something you felt about yourself that you didn't know. It may sound a little abstract, especially when reading the symbol, but it is easier in practice.

Let us get into the exercises now. You don't have to fit all of them into your life, just the ones that you think you would like to, and maybe ones you resist, also. And you don't have to do the introspective parts all the time or the symbol work; use them when you feel like you want answers about yourself or how you view the world.

Writing:

The first modality that we are going to take a look at is writing. This is a little more direct, hence why I put it first. The point of writing is to get your thoughts and feelings out of your system on pen and paper, solidifying what you thought into a verbal, tangible object. When our thoughts are in our heads, it can be difficult to see them, let alone manage them. For example, if you have an idea that you're working on, it can be hard to track all your thoughts. Writing it out gives it structure; you can put it in bullet points, or draw a diagram, or highlight certain things. That is the process of formalizing it. Similarly, you can write about any kind of mental phenomena.

The first exercise we'll talk about is the morning pages, from Julia Cameron. It is supposed to be a practice that is done every day in the morning before you start your day. Get a notebook and pen; you may need a few by the end of the year. Take a few deep breaths and settle down. Start writing whatever comes to your mind for three straight pages in your notebook. It may seem like a lot at first, but just keep your hand moving. The idea is to not pause and think about what you're writing, but to just write whatever comes, and since you've practiced presence, you know there are always thoughts. Avoid judging your writing. This is not about writing a piece of work like a story or a poem; this is just a brain dump, and it is okay to make spelling or grammatical errors. If you can't think of anything, write that down repeatedly; that's okay. It isn't meant to be read by anyone. You don't have to rush; just keep the ship sailing. When you're done, just take a second to relax again.

You really have to do it to feel the effects of the work yourself. Your mind gets cleared by the end of it for the day to come, reducing anxiety and improving mood through presence, and you may get creative ideas. Or you may find surprising things in your writing, like insight into a problem you were having recently. Maybe you'll happen upon some thought and try to question and reframe that thought. The morning pages are a good way to step out of your inhibitions and blocks, and stuckness. It is a practice you can maintain whichever path of life you're on.

A more consciously driven exercise is to keep up a kind of journal for specific things. I journal about how to handle thoughts and feelings as they come up. I use writing as a space to communicate with myself and also problem-solve. "I know that you're feeling troubled, but why don't we try to do a meditation to release this feeling now, and work on our music? Maybe we can try to play some drums with the keyboard.". Writing to myself tells me what I want to hear from my caring, practical adult self, and helps regulate my emotions in that state. Maybe it might just be about writing an idea, like writing the outline to this one you're reading. You can keep journals for. Just how your day went, it is nice to look back later and see how far you've come. Maybe you could even turn it into a blog if you fancy.

You could also write as if you were sending a letter to someone. As corny as it is, it can help you process your relationship with that other person. When people are long gone for whatever reason, this may be the only way that you can talk to them. The point of the exercise is for you to have closure, to express all the things you were not able to express to the other, love, resentment, kindness, sorrow, anything.

What kind of letter would you send to Mimi? She asks you to make it a secret. She wants to be surprised.

A more fun writing exercise is to take a writing prompt from Reddit or somewhere and then write a story or a poem, or a play using that line they provide. Remember, we're not looking to write the next Murakami novel! All we want to do is write without much thinking as to how the story is going to be. For example, once I used a prompt about somebody playing basketball, and then I turned that into a short story where a velociraptor plays one-on-one with the protagonist. That's pretty sick to me, honestly. So just write and see where your creative mind leads you. You could try writing poetry with structure, like a haiku: "You are here to heal. But we are out of cheetos. No roses, no thorns". I don't have a clue as to what that means, but that's the kind of nonsense you just want to embrace. Fitting the stresses and rhymes of a poem can be a fun exercise. And perhaps you'll want to share it at some point.

One short suggestion: try to consciously write about what is on your mind that you are not saying in real life. There are places where we might not be honest with others or ourselves, so take the effort to be authentic in the writing. It is not going to hurt you. All the things unsaid, put it down for your sake, you're allowed to do that, even if it doesn't sound nice. My personal opinion is that the more you accept your mind, pleasant or unpleasant, good or bad, the easier life feels. This is true for any of the exercises.

Visual Art:

Our next modality is about what art typically refers to: paintings, sketches, coloring, collage, and installations. This is going to be more subtle than writing, but can be quite direct as well, depending on what your taste lies in, like how some people draw Still Life while others do Abstract works. Both may contain symbols that you can draw complex meaning from, and they both have value to the viewer. Feel free to modify any exercises to your medium of choice.

For our first exercise, grab a sheet of paper and some colouring materials. Ground yourself before you start drawing, and be open. Either pick a topic you want to study, or keep an open mind about receiving any kind of information. It'll be easier to have a topic in the beginning. Pick up a brush or crayon or whatever you're using and start drawing on the page without stopping to think, just like the writing exercises, it is based on feel, from the unconscious. Put down any shapes, colours, and patterns that come up in your body or mind. It takes a little practice to be uninhibited, but try your best to just move, and you'll enjoy it. Try to catch moments where you feel any particular sensation or some thought comes to mind, it may be related to what you are drawing. There are no rules here, no mistakes, just draw til you feel like you have done enough, or maybe set a timer for 15 minutes. For you, being done might be the whole page, for others it just might be a central object, or maybe it is just lines, squiggles, and polka dots in different colors. Due to it being open-ended, you might have difficulty with momentum, but just draw randomly, like you're just a toddler.

The next step is to take a good look at the piece and start relating. You can note down thoughts on another paper. Here, and for other expressive tasks, you want to ask some of the following questions about the work, such as

- What would I title this?
- What does this painting remind me of?
- What meaning does it have?
- If it had something to say, what things would it tell me? What message does it have? (images speak!)
- What parts of me are you?
- What elements do I feel drawn to? Shape, color.
- Am I feeling anything when I look at this?

- What did I feel while drawing this?
- Anything surprising? Anything made me resist?
- Is there anything I want to change?
- Is there something the piece needs?
- What is not being shown? Negative space.

Like in the last chapter, engage in some dialogue with the answers that come to mind and see where it leads you. Maybe you might find that the colours you used are under-saturated, and that might mean your life is a little drab and dreary. To another, it might be that you're not feeling all of your emotions. So perhaps you can question why you feel this way, and offer something to yourself, like going out for something on the weekend. Check with your personal significance to the shapes, colours, characters, and background, and then you may amplify it by checking out the role of those elements' general meanings in culture, folklore, mythology, stories, like circles representing wholeness.

Mimi leaves a trail of purple paw prints to contemplate. There aren't many capybara artists; she could make it big with her bold statements.

One exercise is to do the same as above, but draw a mandala. Get a compass and draw a circle, and feel free to divide it into two, four, six, or eight parts for symmetry. Design the mandala however you like, paint it in with any kind of medium, tie it up, and ask your questions (The ones from the first exercise). The mandala represents the Self, the totality of your conscious and unconscious mind, so it may be a good exercise to understand how you are displaying different parts of yourself. Instead of journaling alone, you could paint a small mandala every day and talk to it to understand where you may be lacking wholeness today. Are you blocking something? You could also get mandala coloring books and use those as prompts in some sense; you have a base image that means something to you, and how you color is your elaboration of the concept. Coloring books are a great way to self-regulate as well, if you need to.

Another exercise is to make collages, or what are called moodboards, to represent how you feel about something. It is a way of expressing by juxtaposing multiple images, colors, textures, and writing onto one piece of art. Moodboards are used to come up with ideas for how a project should look, but they can be repurposed to examine how we feel. You used to do it by cutting out parts from magazines or newspapers, but we can do it online using Canva or print stickers if you feel compelled to. The idea is to find images that are close to what you feel in your mind; like if I feel like I'm drowning, I might put a picture of a lake that is being battered by rain; I might add a boat tied to the dock; I might put up a house with a lantern in the distance. This might mean to me that there is a safe haven, but it is tough to get there. A lot of blues might signify the evenings for me, which can feel like existential dread. Putting it together gives me a sense of control over what is happening. The elements in the collage might help find more meaning than what you executed for.

The final exercise I'll mention is that you can also meditate on different artworks done by other people. Keep a pen and paper handy, and just stare at the art piece of your choice, welcome the colours and textures, write down any thoughts and feelings that come up, identify what you are putting into the piece from your mind, and trace back their origins. This is similar to using writing prompts; you're using the artwork to stir your internals. You could also draw a counter-piece that follows, opposes, or passes the artwork you are studying. Make up sounds for the artwork, make up movement for the artwork. Don't be afraid to make a little noise.

The process is very subjective and exploratory, so it is hard to give a finer layer of direction. There's no wrong way of doing the work; you will get better at finding your meaning in the painting or sketch, and your line of inquiry will also improve based on insights that you will gain through the process. There are videos on YouTube of people doing art therapy and explaining their thoughts, like IABET Jungian Art. I recommend watching those to get some more ideas on doing inner work with art.

I am including crafts in this category as well. Things like knitting, pottery, and gardening are ways of getting more into the body and in presence. You can create similar exercises for these modalities as well. For example, if you maintain a garden, maybe there is a plant that you talk to for office-related stressors that can be where you store that mental energy. Pottery can be a very sensual experience; it is quite grounding (literally). There is also a sense of mastery that you will develop over time that helps you feel like you've made something happen.

Music:

Like paintings, this modality is more non-verbal, and involves being slightly more in our body than writing or drawing. Along with writing, music is what I have the most experience in, but I find it hard to tap into freely. It feels like I have to let go of my inhibitions to make music work for me again, dropping preconceived notions of what I should be doing and how people will react to it. The notions of should/must and expectation have cast a different light on my relationship with music. This is why I ask that you be open to the exercises even if you have blocks like this. It only changes when we make an attempt to change.

In addition to the internal introspective work, there's an extroverted angle to music. You can write or draw in your space, but with music, at some point, you have the option to play with others and perform, so that can be good for becoming comfortable around others and overcoming performance anxiety.

The first exercise I would like to give is to just sing when you have a space to sing, which might be in the shower. You don't need to be matching on pitch or timing or anything to what you are singing. The only thing you want to do is to sing from your stomach. Typically, people start singing from the throat, which feels a little thin. What you want to do is to push in your stomach when you push out air, singing from your diaphragm. You want your voice to really vibrate in your chest. This stimulates your vagus nerve and helps bring you down to a relaxed state. You can mess around making low-pitched sounds. I find that if I'm singing openly, I'm in a good mood, so that connection means that I can improve my mood just by singing.

And as a bonus, try talking to yourself aloud when you want to think about something. It may seem silly at first, but when I speak aloud, it feels more grounding than keeping it in my head. It is another form of making it tangible, and it can be silly to hear yourself saying "Mythopoesis" out loud.

If Mimi could sing, she would sing some Paramore. "Explain to me, this conspiracy against me."

For the second exercise, composing music can be a very involved process that can be enjoyable as well as grounding. When you have the time, take out 15 minutes to learn how to write music in BeepBox from a YouTube tutorial. Beepbox is a website where you can write down your ideas, and it'll play them back to you. It is a very iterative, feedback-driven process. You just need a little video of somebody else using the software, and you can copy to start with, make random changes, and listen to what you changed. Once you are comfortable, you can take some time in a day to write small looping musical ideas that you come up with, just like in free writing or painting. The idea is to just experiment and see what kind of sounds you can come up with. It's not about writing an actual song; it's about developing a piece of your mind. You could write lyrics over top of it if you feel inclined. Apply our questions to what you've made and see what comes up.

My primary way of writing music is to toss in some seed ideas, maybe a few chords, and listen to what I want to hear next. If I'm playing the guitar, I'll listen to where a melody wants to go, and there could be several places. For all you know, that might correspond to various choices in your life.

Like artwork, you can sit down and listen to a piece of music, the different instrumental layers, the space, the pace at which it moves, the lyrical meaning, if any, or just sit back and enjoy João Gilberto. What does this particular track mean to you?

Like moodboards, you can make playlists for how you're feeling. Maybe only Weird Fishes/Arpeggi is the response you have when people ask how you're feeling today. It can be a way to capture errant feelings in the air.

If possible, you can invest some money and time into learning an instrument, and spend some time each week to just mess around, play some song parts. A musical instrument is a companion that you can have for a lifetime; it could be something small like a harmonica or a kalimba. If you love what you're messing around with, you will naturally get better as a musician, seeking out technique and execution to expand your abilities and what you can make possible. Eventually, you will be able to play with other musicians, which can add to your fulfillment if that speaks to you.

One last offering I'll leave you with is that you can create your own musical rituals that you can conduct for some kind of purpose. Perhaps there are a few lines you would like to hum that you can perform in the morning as a note of gratitude towards the break of dawn and being here another day. Maybe there's a small lullaby xylophone melody you can play before bed to indicate it is time to sleep and move into the dream world.

Movement:

I am as graceful as a drunk monkey, but I've found that movement can be a really good way to self-regulate and process your deepest thoughts without having to say much at all. It can be useful as another body-based approach for releasing stuck emotions. I only have one exercise to offer, but you could come up with your own at this point.

Back during the COVID lockdown in 2020, I was in a particularly dark place and in a quest for some spiritual help. One night, I was just walking in my room in the dark, and I started listening to some songs, I think by Advaita. And something prompted me to just dance around, like I knew Indian classical, and I just sort of parroted slow movements without really knowing what I was doing. I just swayed and turned and stretched like a tree in the wind, or perhaps like how Kundalini would move me. I cannot remember how it felt afterwards, but it felt very meaningful, like I had processed something I didn't even know. There were just vibes, for lack of a better word. Move when you need to self-regulate, or when you want to process a certain emotion. Maybe you could create your own dance language through gestures that you can rely on to "speak". Something very universal about that.

It can feel silly to dance. You may think you look ridiculous. But hey, you're at home, this is just for you. Go all out.

Mimi goes to the Mammalian Discotheque every so often to dance to Squarepusher.

Psychodrama:

Now, the use of theatre in the context of healing is something I have next to no knowledge on, but I am a little familiar with the idea of what a psychodrama as I've participated in a few, so I thought I would share an experience and leave the rest for you to explore.

In 2023, I had the pleasure of participating in a shamanism workshop where I learned some beautiful teachings. My friend, the facilitator, would launch into psychodramas when he sensed that somebody had an inhibiting thought or behavior; he had an eye for it. So, to explore the inner world of the person, we would take different roles in their internal worlds. The central person would play themselves, while others would play their emotions like a constriction in the throat, or endurance against pain. He would talk to the personified feelings, and others would reflect their words back to him.

This gives an opportunity for the person to review his thoughts, and how he feels, and the facilitator would guide improvisational questions in between, trying to lead the person to a meeting ground of some kind between their inhibition and freedom. Sometimes we would say what the person may be feeling to help them think. We might mime some kind of actions. The whole process allows for some distance between the person and his inner voices, allowing them to engage without being overwhelmed. At the end of it, all of us would be released from our roles by the central person. I had a particularly difficult time with this because I don't want to reveal my inner world completely, but we got to something useful, which is that I have voices/inner characters that are not mine dictating how I should live life, and my own is subdued. My path became about finding my own voice, which I'm currently on, as well as trusting my own experience.

Hopefully, you get an idea as to how elements of drama can be used to examine the inner world. Definitely requires a facilitator, not something I would say you should do on your own. Even with a facilitator, it can get rough.

Film:

Photography and Videography are stirring ways of expression; they allow you to capture and present reality in your own perspective (literally), in a way that is unique and involves delicacy and care. The process of taking a photograph, from identifying a subject to composition to capture, is meticulous, and almost becomes zen-like in its approach. There are stories you can pick up from a photograph, potentialities you can pull on to create a story. Videos, even more so, are designed to be a medium of storytelling. One of my favorite parts of movie making is how you can capture so many things through a single shot, the mood, the intensity, subtle meaning in the objects, and a casual action by the actor that gives way so much about character and the scene. At its apex, cinema is a holy communion between visual art, music, writing, dramatics, and other expressions. Makes it a good place to see how you integrate.

Mimi is preparing for her big role in your biopic about yourself. She gets her makeup kit.

The first exercise I would like you to do is to make some time in the day, maybe while commuting, to capture photos of whatever catches your eye. Don't worry about composition or exposure; maybe you can put it on auto. Just aim and shoot. It can be a small moment of presence, to just acknowledge the existence of a bus stand or graffiti. Later, look back at your photos and choose one you feel compelled to look at, and just write down the elements of the photo, what you see, and what is outside the frame.

Ask yourself if there is a reason why you took this photo; is there something communicated? You can ask the open questions from the previous sections. Maybe there's a memory that comes up that you want to examine.

The continuation of this exercise is to load the photo up in an editing software and play around with the controls. You could use Snapseed if your phone supports it. Ask yourself how you want the photo to look. Do you want to convey a message, a mood? Put some filters on, change contrast, blur, and add text, whatever it is, so it is more like what you see in your head. Maybe you want to make the darker blue shadows stand out more, or bring some warmth into it. When you're done, compare and contrast the two photos and see if it brings up some thoughts, like why I want to make this change. What does it remind me of? You may access deep desires and changes you want to happen.

Of course, you can also just shoot and edit and have a present, fun time. It can just be a meditative experience, as are the other modalities.

Similarly, you can make small home movies out of videos you capture, and also stock videos that you get online. You can use Davinci and cut and splice videos together to create some kind of narrative and sync it to some music that you like, edit in sounds, voice-overs, and pictures. You don't need an end goal in mind, just maybe like a three-minute video. You can color grade the videos, like you did for photos in the last exercise. This can be thought of as a space-time mandala, integrating different parts into one unified whole. Ask yourself why you made the decisions that you did, and what this video story is telling you. What outcome did the project have emotionally?

You can also try to use writing prompts to weave a video, or you could capture a photo for a "job", like a restaurant magazine asked you to review them. You may be more limited, but restrictions can bring out unexpected creativity.

Identification:

One of the most crucial events that happens during the consumption of artistic material is the identification of one's own parts with objects in the art, that is, we are seeing ourselves reflected in the medium. That is why creative content is so important; we want something that we can relate to, connect to, and share ourselves. We dive into stories seeking ourselves and looking for greater meaning, for understanding, whether it's conscious or not. For instance, I find myself drawn to Debussy's Claire De Lune, because it captures some part of me that is wistful and yet optimistic. I feel as if I'm in some Victorian living room waiting to meet my estranged daughter, bittersweet. What this means for me, I have to sit down and explore what needs I am looking to meet. But it makes me feel seen. Next time, when you identify with something, a character, a scene, or dialogue, ask yourself what it is that you are drawn to? What is the connection? Also, what is it you feel averse about? These things reveal our values and principles, how we respond to pain, our limitations, and may help you make meaning in your life. A heart made fullmetal.

The process of identification is healing for all sorts of people. A dear friend of mine seems to get insights about himself and the world often from content like FFXIV or DnD streams. We say that fiction is his scripture, as he finds these kernels of truth present in the material, for example, the idea of being a Paladin, to protect and speak truth. That builds his own sense of justice and kindness. Use the media as a way to engage with yourself and broaden your horizons. Of course, there are times when you will feel connected to less morally glamorous material, but that is okay too; we're respecting the totality of our mind. We have a choice over our actions and who we choose to be.

This goes without saying, but consumption of art and the world is really important for your inner work as well. You want to restock the pantry with new and engaging material that you not only identify with, but also gives you new ideas to play with. For example, if you are engaged with a baby or children, your mind might be trying to express yourself in a way children can understand, and that will reflect in your work. Your relationships with people will also bleed into it, whether pleasant or not; it's okay. Find new things to do, people to meet; these things are good for your mental health as well as your creative health. As difficult as it may be, those first steps will make things easier to do again and again.

This is the end of this chapter. You should now feel more like a creative and a purveyor of symbols. Take your time with the exercises you choose to engage with; they benefit from sincere practice, and you'll find ideas that you can translate between modalities as well. This turned out to be a lot longer than I expected; it just goes to show you the intricacy of artwork.

Be curious.

Mimi jumped around at the sight of all the fanfare at the Renaissance Gathering. There were so many artisans, so much art, and theatre, and music, and pinhole cameras, what a wonderful affair. Each booth asks you to take part in their merry-making. You and Mimi end up being covered in orange paint and clay, learning songs you've never heard from ancient poets, and the science of astronomy. At night, you reflect on all that you did, while Mimi snores away. It has been a long time since you played like this.

✦✦✦

CHAPTER 5

SACRED SPACE

In the last chapter, we were introduced to the unconscious, symbol work, and listening for what it has to say in the scope of creative expression. It is something that is felt and intuitive instead of a rational thinking process. You sat ready for the art to tell you what it thinks and believes, and feels. Inner child work is another space where you listen, you interact with a part of your psyche, adult to child, and reparent the hurt part of you. In the end, you are an integrated being, a sum of parts, a gestalt, but there is a world inside of you that consists of many characters and objects, and landscapes. When you draw a pond and fish, there is an image in the mind you draw out, a living image that is alive to engage with. Those fish are breathing within your consciousness.

In this chapter, we are going to take the idea of the unconscious and its parts further, and turn to exploring our inner worlds in different ways. Healing is not about fixing, but more about meeting, relating. The task is to grow, to be reminded of your wholeness. This is about digging deep, and that may be big healing, but also very provoking — shame, grief, and fear, so be aware of your tolerance and disengage when you feel it is too much. That is just part of the process; the unconscious is a helper/messenger, and you have the first two chapters to hold you.

My own experiences with the kind of inner work we're going to engage with have been of merit; it felt like I had found something in me that was there all along, waiting to be explored. It brought another dimension to life, not something drastic, but quiet and potent. I felt more aligned with myself, stepping into being an intronaut. It seems that I am urged to engage with the deeper parts of me. I would like it if it brings this same depth to you, this little gift. Like always, it is your experience that shows you the benefit of the methods.

I once had a dream when I was around 12-13 years old, that I was standing on top of an ocean with dark clouds above. A giant abandoned and wrecked pirate ship was floating in the sky, glowing electric blue, and it was named the Arcanum. I didn't know what it meant, so I went to school and looked it up in a dictionary to find it meant "a deep, mysterious secret", which was apt. Maybe I should've known then that I'd be dealing with an introspective life. If you feel this in your bones, then you know what the heart of the chapter is.

So, we are going to take this gently. I'm going to introduce you to three methods of working with the unconscious mind. Let's look at a therapy modality first that is akin to Inner Child work.

Parts Work:

The most well known kind of parts work is Internal Family Systems (IFS), a modality that has picked up a lot of steam in the evidence-based therapy circles, which is quite effective at managing trauma through dialogue with the inner family. Richard C Schwartz came up with this method over several sessions, where he noticed clients talking about having parts, "Oh that part of me doesn't like that, part of me is telling met to do this", and he dialogued with these parts through the client and figured out he could help the clients by talking to and helping the parts, which took some trial and error. He applied family dynamics to figure out the roles and relationships between parts and guided the clients to resolve issues such as bulimia through the unburdening of the parts. In IFS, the parts have roles to play in keeping the system going, but perhaps in a dysfunctional way, that's their burden. They are formed in childhood when needs are unmet, or if an adverse experience happens. Changing the dynamics between parts and client heals the system.

Now that being said, we're not going to use IFS in its standard form, but instead, we are going to follow a slightly different process that makes things a little more organic and open and less clinical by removing the categorization of parts. It doesn't take away from the heart of the work, and the process is very similar. I switched to this style after a dear friend of mine told me about how she does parts work with her clients. I found this a little more suitable to my mind, but if you would like to stick to what the regular IFS approach is, please read "No Bad Parts" by Richard C Schwartz. You can also watch videos on YouTube where he demonstrates IFS sessions with different YouTubers.

We try to work from the place of the Self, which is the part of us that is calm, connected, confident, curious, courageous, compassionate, clear, and creative. In his sessions, Richard found that everyone talked about this one part when they were in a resourceful place. We are going to try and work from this place when we talk to parts. When we are not in that space, we are said to be merged or blended with a part, so we take on its emotions, and we are controlled by that part. For example, when we feel afraid, we are channeling the energy of a part that is scared of something. By doing the exercises from chapter one, you can stay in your Self, unblended from the part that's afraid, so that we can interact with that part from a stable space. Our earlier chapters should've prepared you to wield all the Cs. You don't have to completely be in Self to do parts work. Even if it is only ten percent, that is fine.

Okay, let's get into the actual work.

When you do parts work, you can choose a feeling, a thought, or a behavior that you want to examine. You can close your eyes and meditate for a minute if you'd like. Gently ask for the part that carries the feeling, thought, or behavior, like "Hey, could the worrying part please talk to me?" and let it show up in any way, as an image or sensation, or thought. For example, my worrying part is Courage the Cowardly Dog, he's worried about everything all the time. I can see him screaming in my head. If you feel too much emotion, ask the part to step back from you so you can talk to it properly. Chances are that the part will listen to you, and you will feel calmer.

Ask it questions like what it's feeling, what it's thinking about, when it started worrying, what would happen if it didn't worry, and engage in dialogue like this. Treat it like it's a person, and try to really understand and be there for the part. For example, Courage told me he had to keep baking cakes to feed the monsters, that was his way of keeping the scary things at bay. So then, I would ask it what it needs, and try to help it fulfil that need or something similar, on a doable level. Courage just wants to be on my lap. Be compassionate with the part. Let it know you're here to take care of it and that you can handle responsibility, the part can be **unburdened**, it can trust you to handle the system, especially from Self. Show it that it doesn't need to worry anymore and that you have control, it can do something else instead of worrying, like enjoy a good vacation in the Maldives.

If it's hesitant to talk to you, work with you, that's okay, we can do this over time. You can come back to this part the next day and show that you are reliable and can be trusted. The parts can be really young, depending on when it was initiated, like maybe you started worrying from the age of three. The age it is will affect the dynamics as well. How would you talk to a child that young when they're having trouble?

When you make contact and treat the part with care, you will find your emotions settling down, and you'll be more in line with your Self. That's how you know it really has an impact.

You can repeat this exercise with the other parts that you will find in daily life, like angry parts, grieving parts, lethargic parts, resistant parts, hopeless parts, and shameful parts. Be with the angry part, let it know it's okay to be mad, talk it through its feelings and thoughts, and see if you can figure out what they need, maybe you need to change how you have been doing things. Funnily, if you're feeling sleepy during a conversation, it might be a part that makes you sleepy, so that you can avoid a tricky subject. Try to maintain a list or a visual map of your different parts, and visit them from time to time to see how they are doing. That keeps S elf-leadership alive, and they know they can rely on you.

Don't forget to visit Mimi either, or she's going to be mad at you for a little bit.

Now, these parts may end up having issues with one another. Like, let's say you have a worrying part, you may find yourself being angry at that part, which is another part that is angry that the worrying part is causing problems. Maybe it is your inner critic showing up. In those cases, talk to them separately. Ask the angry part to step back and go into a waiting space, like a room or a garden, or a temple. Talk to the worrying part and address its issues, then bring back the angry part and show that things are okay now. Then you may want to talk to the angry part. Be thankful to both parts for being involved. So this practice is essentially being your own therapist employed by all your parts. Where's my cheque?

Feel free to modify the steps you take to talk to your parts. This is the typical approach in IFS, and there's this structured dialogue that helps you direct focus to unburdening and healing. The pseudoscript shows you to engage and be friendly with the part, find out what it's responsible for, what it believes, why it does what it does, and how you can help it. Those are the key points to remember and address, but you can talk to it however you see fit. All in all, it is a very simple process and quite effective, yet deeply introspective.

For another example, I had a part that was waiting for things to happen; job changes, relationship status, mental health, creative recognition, and it turned out it was Le Quack, and the trick was to keep me waiting so that I wouldn't be overwhelmed by the feeling of the uncertainty of the future. I kept waiting and holding on to hope, but at this point, it was giving me more pain than hope. So we talked and I gave him the job of being in the present moment and hoping for love and joy, a quality instead of an event. He was hesitant, but is taking it up slowly. My day-to-day became less about the wait and trying to enjoy moments in it, though it's a serious WIP.

Finally, consider taking the symbolic angle and dissecting what a part means to you. What does Courage represent for me? A caretaker who wants to keep their close ones safe goes to great lengths, bravely. That shows me the positive aspects of the part, which is also myself, and I feel great kinship with Courage. You can also take up your creative expression with these parts; you could draw your parts, write entries or dialogue between parts, and give musical qualities to the parts, movement, and voices like they are puppets. They are all ways of further integrating them. Take your time to work through this one and see how the shoe fits. Parts work is such that you blend the power of symbols with the day-to-day, so it doesn't feel too abstract and out there, but at the same time provides depth into your psyche.

Dream Work:

The second method of inner work in this chapter has to do with dreams, rich with symbolism, a direct product of the unconscious mind. Our dreams can be a way of understanding ourselves; our motives, our failings, our wants and needs, and what is in balance. Jung believed that dreams were messages from both the personal unconscious and the greater collective unconscious, which we are all tied to, using symbols as shorthand for intricate meaning. Dreams are a means to help the dreamer achieve individuation, the process of becoming whole. It shows us how to balance the see-saw of psychic qualities, like our stances toward success and failure, of somehow maintaining samabodhi, equanimity to both.

So, for us, we will briefly talk about the interpretation of dreams.

Generally, we may remember only one or two dreams over the course of a night's sleep; the rest is forgotten. When you wake up from a dream, do not make sudden moves; slowly reach out for your phone or a notebook and record what happened in the dream. Moving quickly erases the dream. Later, when you get time to come back to the dream, consult the entry. To go back and read improves your dream recall for the next day. Affirming that you will dream before going to bed also helps recall.

When interpreting, you first want to get the general transit of the dream; what was happening in the dream, what things interacted together, what was your role in the dream, and what changed. Were you just spectating? Did the forest turn into a city? Try to capture fine details like mood, colour, space, sounds, you never know what could trigger insight. Write down how you felt about the different aspects of the dream. Use the prompt "This aspect made me feel like…". For example, seeing my family in the dream made me feel uncomfortable. Maybe there was an argument, and you felt uneasy. What is it about the family that makes you uncomfortable? Do you feel like there is distance? Take that aspect and tease out the symbolic meaning of the elements in that scene and their connections. For family, it may be that I don't feel connected to my roots, my home, or maybe there are unresolved familial tensions. Family doesn't have to be your literal family, but what the idea represents; for example, close connections. There is no right way to interpret a dream; there is no need to understand everything. This is your reading of it based on your personal meaning, and what's important are the feelings you are left with, your intuitive sense, and what you are supposed to know now. You can then do a second pass of the dream with collective meaning, and symbolism you find in stories, religious, or spiritual traditions, and artwork. There could be universal patterns (archetypes) like the wise old man or the mother. You can put the personal and collective together to get a wider narrative. Symbol meaning may differ from context to context, so the interpretation will also depend on who you are as well as your current context. If you are under a lot of work stress, the dream may show you how to balance that. Ask yourself if the dream material is compensating for something, trying to bring balance.

If it's a longer dream, you may want to take it scene by scene, and see how things change between them. If a person with you changes to somebody else, examine what qualities have changed with the exchange of these people. The people may be actual people in your life, or they could be symbolic as well. For example, one's mother could be about your own caretaking and motherhood. If the scene goes from day to night, then what was the transition about, what quality changed between day and night, was it certainty to uncertainty? Our dreams are often about what is happening in the present, memory consolidation, and not so much the past and future. So you could narrow down some interpretations that way. Pick the interpretation that feels the most true to you, even if unpleasant.

When you think you've done enough digging, put together the story of what the dream was about for you personally, what you felt was important, and what impact the dream has on you in ordinary reality. Integrate the dream through acts in the real world, practical as well as symbolic. This helps the work sink in.

For example, I had a dream a few days ago where I was in my house and I was sitting under a skylight. Two eagles circled ahead and kept tossing large sticks into my house. In the dream, I was afraid, and it seemed the eagles were attacking me, trying to chase me out of their territory, displaying aggressive behavior. I had a boomerang with me for defense. Personally, eagles symbolize confidence and power, and collectively, wise and free, so it seemed like a strong force wanted to occupy where I stayed. It could be that my home, my sense of self, provides a warm and safe place for the eagles, but I am an outsider in part. It may be that a part of me seems to be a threat in the system. This makes a lot of sense for me as I am going through a tumultuous period where I'm not taking care of myself. Yet there is something new that needs to be nurtured. They bring strong qualities, but they need this negligent part of me to step aside. The boomerang signifies a sort of deterrent rather than a weapon, my resistance, saying that this is my space. This conflict is one interpretation of the dream; there could be other things I'm not seeing right now. The action I would take is to think about how I can allow for these strong qualities to enter my life. Maybe I have to show that I am the home to the eagles.

This should have given you an understanding of what dream work is like. You could read more about it in "Man & His Symbols" by Jung, or just watch a few videos on YouTube to get a sense of how to do it, what to ask. Interpretation becomes natural rather quickly. The most important thing is to translate them into action, or it just remains an intellectual exercise, which is fun, but the dream asks more of us. It wants us to stabilize the scales.

Mimi is not sure what a dream is. Both reality and dreams sound the same to her.

A continuation of dream work in reality is possible through the practice of **Active Imagination**, which is the process of relating and communicating with the various figures or objects, or scenes in the dream, to better understand the dream, peel layers, or extend it. Of course, this seems quite similar to parts work, except that the source is from your dreams, and that you are dialoging more freely with fewer prescribed steps. It is more about open exploration, interpretation, and insight rather than consoling and unburdening parts, although both lead to healing in their own ways. It can feel more like daydreaming reveries with a strong intent to interact. Parts work can feel more grounded as there's a smaller fraction of unconscious content to handle.

The active imagination process is like how we drew meaning from artwork; you ask questions, talk to the dream object, and listen for responses. For example, I may talk to my eagles to see what they are trying to establish in my home, and they may reply that this is where their home used to be. This could indicate that they used to be part of my home system, but were evicted for some reason. Maybe I lost all my confidence and power when I was small. I was trained in helplessness, unable to trust my own experience. So now, the eagles and I may have an understanding. Go back to the last scene and see if the dream continues as images, sounds, sensations, maybe there is more for you to see. Keep yourself open and curious towards the dream, and accept what may come your way. Remember, at the end, tie it back to something actionable, and integrate. Take it slow, don't rush to find a meaning; sometimes insights may come to you days apart.

Also, you can engage in active imagination outside of dream elements as well, just like how you engage in parts work.

Since I've presented dream work and active imagination, which come from Jungian work, I would be remiss if I did not add an entry about **shadow work.**

The shadow is the part of your unconscious where all your repressed emotions lie, which happened as a result of parental and societal conditioning, fear of rejection, and trauma, the parts of you that are shut down to be an ideal self. To be a "good" girl, you may have had to stuff down certain qualities to be ladylike, which means suppressing your emotions, like your anger or sadness, and had to be quiet and subservient to others. They are rejected and stowed away. These shadow parts of you grow to become large and unwieldy, and your emotional stability will take a hit for putting them under wraps for so long. The imbalance builds over time and in moments of little provocation, the shadow part may come out and lash out violently, causing harm to yourself and others. The shadow naturally appears by projecting onto others;

we see our own shortcomings in other people, and that is how we can recognize our own shadow parts. What we are repulsed by, we have in ourselves, otherwise we would not recognize.

Jung believed the psyche had to be in balance, so these shadow parts need nurturing and reintegration into the system. Robert A Johnson writes that for each action there is a shadow in its place to balance the seesaw psyche, so there must be some methods to ensure that the shadow is honoured, such as small rituals, like drawing from the shadow, or dialogue to understand and care for the shadow part. The idea behind shadow work is not to reject societal norms and to act on violent impulses or manipulation, but to acknowledge and accept their existence within you, and additionally find the gold lining. For example, manipulation in a more refined sense can be seen as persuasion, which can be a good thing to carry, otherwise lost in the exile of the shadow.

For a personal example, if I don't like bossy people, it is a reflection that I am averse to bossiness in myself, and I shut it down to be accepted by others. But in my bossiness is the trait of creating structure and order, which can be a good thing for me to help others with. That's the helpful part. In dream work and active imagination, you may encounter your shadow parts often, hence why we talk about it. I've encountered a black panther once in my dreams, who came up to me with no fear, embodying strength and quiet confidence that I, too, should embody in real life. I've shut down being bold and authoritative to keep away from conflict, but maybe it is time I spoke up. In this case, my shadow is not an outright negative aspect; it could be seen as noble. We may have repressed that which is beneficial. You can encounter the shadow in dreams, parts work, expressive work, or in other people. Working with the shadow leads us to individuation; the widening of the consciousness and movement towards wholeness, holding the opposites in peace.

We've now seen parts work and the Jungian approach. There is one more approach I would like to talk about, which also calls for deep inner change.

Shamanism:

I mentioned in the last chapter that I had attended a shamanism workshop in 2023. That experience was important for me to open myself up to this archetype of healing, of entering the inner world and engaging with it from a deep and sacred space. It was only later that I engaged in parts work and Jungian work. Here we'll be talking about a few things that I learned at that time and later outside of that space. This is the most out-there concept in the book, but read a bit and you'll see that it might make sense to you.

Shamanism is an ancient way of interacting with the spirit world/non-ordinary reality to seek help with issues in ordinary reality, which has roots in centuries-old indigenous practices of various shamanic groups, fit for healing, divination, and insight through practices and stories. For example, the healer of a community, like the šamán of the Tungus people, would have rituals with drumming, chanting, and singing where they would invite the spirits and have dialogue with them to solve problems, like finding a source for food and water. People who were sick were seen to have an illness spirit with them, who could be persuaded to leave the host through ritual and gifts. A person who was able to do these accurately became the spokesperson/shaman for that group. You don't choose to be, you are initiated. We would just be practitioners, dabblers otherwise.

The core belief of many groups with a spiritual healer is that of animism, that everything in nature has a spirit. The shaman knows how to communicate with them, such as learning about plants with medicinal value. They know how to translate between realms and mediate. One could talk to the spirit of the land to know what it has seen, what the history of the land is. They tune into the phases of the moon and the seasons to see what the celestials have to say. It is a very intuitive way of life. In a modern context, we could still ask these questions, ask for healing of our body, mind, spirit, and guidance for our problems, or understanding/exploring the world of Spirit. Nature is our ally, and we respectfully ask for guidance.

My personal belief is that the psyche precedes matter in the universe, and all matter and energy arise from it. Everything does have a spirit in this place of the psyche, which exists outside of space and time. The more tuned we are to the collective unconscious, the closer we are to this field of play, and our world arises from it like waves in an ocean. It is what Dr. Brand in Interstellar refers to as love being a meaningful signal when they talk about going to Edmund's planet. In this context, it seems rather fitting that we can talk to the spirits; they could be psychic beings rather than material beings, but also could manifest materially. Anyway, that's my metaphysical take I put out there for consideration, because from this frame it looks very similar to what we were doing already, talking to psychical parts, psychical figures, and objects. Perhaps shamanism is also parts work and active imagination from a more sacred, reverent, universal frame, knowing that we are all interconnected.

Mimi nods solemnly as if to acknowledge this connection between worlds.

There is a lot to capture when it comes to shamanic work, so I will just take you through a few basic practices to get you started. For further work, I recommend that you read books by the wonderful teacher Sandra Ingerman to get yourself more acquainted with what shamanism is like now. You could start with 'Shamanic Journeying' and go to 'Awakening to the Inner World'. I will leave it up to you to consider her books and choose something that feels meaningful to you. Her videos on YouTube are also very informative and practical, so you could start there as well. Again, integration is important.

So, we're going to plan to go to the spirit world to meet a few spirits who will be helpful for further journeys. Journeying refers to going into the spirit world. I need to explain some concepts. The cosmology of the spirit world is that most of it exists in non-ordinary reality, and we exist within a portion of this, like a Matryoshka, called ordinary reality. There is a spiritual layer in our reality called the Middle world, it is like a twin version made of spirit. Other than that, there is the Lower world, which is of forests, deserts, mountains, nature, animals, plant guides, and there is the Upper world, which is mostly composed of light objects like clouds, crystals, spirit guides, and teachers. This distinction is fluid and on a spectrum in nature, but it helps our work to break it into three, initially for structure. We could start with the lower world. I'll tell you why.

Each person is said to draw their strength from what is referred to as a power animal. This animal represents its entire species, and is said, in some cultures, to be with you since birth. Sometimes they change. Some people have more than one power animal. The lower world is where power animals reside. So it seems rather fitting to go and meet and honor this power animal that has been with you for so long, protecting you, silently guiding you. Maybe it's Hawk or Gazelle or Crocodile. They aren't a hawk or the hawk, but Hawk, the representative of the species.

Before we journey, we have to identify what our axis mundi, the central axis of the world, is. This is where our journeys typically start. So sit down, take a few deep breaths and settle, and when you're ready, ask that you be shown a tree to be your axis mundi. Different people get messages in different ways. We've talked about getting images, sounds, and sensations before, so when you journey, you may not see images clearly but hear sounds. I tend to see images, so I will refer to the messages as images. When you ask for a tree, multiple images may come up for you, but try to pick out the one that stands out in your mind, that feels like something. Remember this tree and its surrounding location, you will use this place to start your journeys. Take a few minutes to talk to the tree, let it know you are here, ask it how old it is, and what wisdom it has for you before you begin this larger journey of doing spirit work.

We have that ready now. When we journey, we do so with the help of drums, rattles, chanting, and maybe singing. Typically, a drum is repetitively beaten at the same speed as theta waves in the brain, which indicate dreaming. It is likely you don't have a drum, so you can use a 10-15 minute drum track on YouTube uploaded from Michael Harner's material. You can do some singing to invite your power animal. The drum track will slow down to indicate that the journey is over. Then you can retrace your steps back to the axis mundi, say thanks, and get up from the journey.

So, imagine you are in your axis mundi. Set your intention for this journey; that is what will drive your understanding of the images, sounds, and sensations you will encounter. Your intention is to meet your power animal; repeat it in your head. The entrance to the lower world will be through the bark of the tree, the roots of the tree, a hole in the ground, or a trapdoor. Something that goes down. When you start the drum track, go through this into the lower world.

You will be met with natural landscapes. Follow your natural instinct and walk around. Wait for a power animal to show up. When they do, ask them if they are your power animal. If they are not, continue walking and run into more animals. You will feel it in your heart when something makes sense. If you don't see anybody, repeat your intention and keep going. It may be a creature of fantasy as well, like a Pokémon. If you do meet your power animal, spend some time asking things like what it brings to you, what qualities it shares, whether it has guidance or medicine, and whether there is something you can do for your power animal. When the dream ends, ask your power animal to come with you through the opening you came from. Then you could ask for guidance during waking life. Thank the power animal at the end. If you don't find a power animal, you just have to come back another time; maybe circumstances are not suitable.

My power animal showed up with a loud announcement. I kept seeing animals, but none of them seemed like my power animal, until he finally made a lot of ruckus and introduced himself. So that is an option.

Make sure to integrate your power animal through expression, and make some rituals. For example, I took photos of the sky for my power animal when we first met; he was a type of bird. You could draw yourself and the power animal, and draw a circle of protection. Talk to the power animal from time to time. Embody its qualities. Build a small altar space to do your journeys, in front of which has some objects with symbolic meaning important to you. This is how you make the spiritual work pragmatic and down-to-earth. While you can learn about power animal symbolism online, take time to find your personal significance, you can talk to your power animal to know what they represent. The Jungian way is present here, or perhaps, came from here.

Now that you know how to journey, next time you can go to the lower world with your power animal for some kind of guidance on a problem in ordinary reality, and that can come from your power animal or another entity in nature, other animals, plants, trees, rocks, rivers. You can also ask your power animal to help you release or clear wounds and attachments. The other kinds of reasons to journey are for power retrieval, which is to reclaim what you lost by giving your power away to someone else, and soul retrieval. Some cultures believe that your soul splits into fragments when you undergo deep wounding, like trauma, and the shaman goes into the spirit world to retrieve those parts of you that are mainly children. But these are supposed to be done once you have a lot more experience with the spirit world.

The next journey you could do is to visit the upper worlds to meet a teacher, a spiritual guide. You could go to the upper world through the branches of your tree, or through a ladder or rope, or a crack in the sky. You have to go beyond planets and galaxies to reach the soft light world of the upper world. Here you may meet mythical and mystical figures. For instance, I met with Sai Baba of Shirdi and have had him as a guide for future journeys. I've naively done two soul retrievals; his soft presence was beneficial to winning the trust of the wounded children. This is an example of the wise old man archetype coming up in the journey.

After that, you could visit the elements of nature: fire, water, air, and earth. You could talk to the moon to study how the lunar phases affect you.

There is a huge, vast amount of information and practicalities about doing shamanic spirit work that I myself have yet to practice. I can't capture it all here, my intention was to only show you another approach that goes in deeply into the psyche and has a rich history and myths from all over, which makes the symbol work powerful. You can choose whichever method appeals to you, just like all the other exercises in this book. You may choose to bring your spiritual encounters into your parts work and active imagination. Maybe your power animal now helps you engage with your different parts; a scared part can be shown the protection your power animal provides.

Here, we end this chapter, hopefully, this wasn't too overwhelming for you or put you off from doing inner work. Keep an open heart when you can as you work with these modalities. Working with your inner world can be powerful, and making that accessible was one of the other intentions of this chapter. If anything, I hope you get why I called this chapter sacred space.

Be alive.

Mimi takes you through the end of the world, the Forest of Mirrors. This is the last stop on your journey together, and it is confusing. You go from one mirror to another and go around in circles, seeing multiples of you and Mimi. Finally, you take the courage to walk into the mirrors, and the spell dissolves. You and Mimi emerge into a clearing and a lake, with a boat moored to the pier. It is time to leave this behind, you think. Mimi simply points at the center of a lake.

We paddle the boat over. There is a house and a key for me to open it. And it opens to color, to all the other places we have been, and will be. Mimi grunts as if to say, "Let's go".

I walk through the multidimensional portal with her, and we transform into everything; all the colours, all the shapes, all the feelings. Unus mundus.

✦✦✦

ENDING

Thank you for coming with me on this jam-packed journey on handling mental health. It's not an easy thing to make it here, so congratulations, hopefully you've learned many ways of dealing with your problems, and maybe some things beyond that as well. You can come back to the book at any time, on any page. Like I said in the introduction to the book, healing is a spiral; you'll come back to concepts again and again and find yourself in need of reminders.

I hope you make something from each chapter a part of your life. I've mentioned here and there how the practices are related, such as how compassion is central to parts work, and presence helps cope with difficult emotions. So, try to see it as one fluid, dynamic system where all sorts of colours mix to make up your mental healing.

For example, I try to wake up around six in the morning, make some tea, maybe walk, and do some morning pages or journaling. This calms my nervous system down for the day. Over the day, I may check on myself to see how I'm doing, and any parts that need attention. I try to tend to my anxious part often. Later in the evening, maybe I'll cook. I'll make some time for play, I'll play guitar for a bit, or if I feel like drawing, just quickly look for symbols. When I wind down for bed, I search for any residual feelings and where they came from. Soft descent into sleep.

I've tried to include a wide range of exercises and concepts in this book, all the stuff I've used over the course of the last few years, because you never know which one will click with a person. It may feel like a lot, but over weeks, you may ask for more. I hope it genuinely helps you.

This has been a long journey for me. I'm left with grief as these pages come to an end, having to let go and come back to the day-to-day routine. There's uncertainty in how this book will be received, whether I was of help to you, I feel vulnerable having been so open like this, and I seek a sense of meaning to hold onto. The good news is that the book will hold space for me, too, and so will you, as I figure things out and continue on my own journey. Keep me in your prayers.

Be well. Let Mimi be with you.

✦✦✦

APPENDIX FOR EXERCISES

The point of this appendix is to give you brief descriptions of the exercises that are mentioned in each chapter. You should read the chapters to understand the exercises first, and then you can come back here whenever you want to look them up.

Chapter 1: It's all about presence. Use these to stay centered, grounded. Look for a sense of space and openness.

- Ex 1.1: Observe an object in your room. Look for color, texture, and weight.
- Ex 1.2: Bring your attention to your breath as it travels in and out of your body.
- Ex 1.3: Box breathing, 4s inhale, 4s hold, 4s exhale, 4s hold, repeat.
- Ex 1.4: 4-7-8 breathing, 4s inhale, 7s hold, 8s exhale
- Ex 1.5: Sit with the mental phenomena in your mind. Experience thoughts and feelings, but do not hold on to any. Let it come and go. Defusion - you are not the phenomena.

- Ex 1.6: Notice how we judge thoughts and feelings, and let go of that judgement.
- Ex 1.7: 5-4-3-2-1, 5 things you can see, 4 you can hear, 3 you can feel, 2 you or remember smelling, 1 you can taste. Approach it slowly.
- Ex 1.8: Listen for the silence that is beneath all sounds.
- Ex 1.9: Body scan for any and all sensations, name each one.
- Ex 1.11: Jacobson's Progressive Muscle Relaxation.
- Ex 1.12: Do difficult arithmetic.
- Ex 1.13: Recite a story or poem. Recall random facts, question facts. Play a game of Name-Place-Animal-Thing.
- Ex 1.14: Krishnan's RAIN sibling. Recognize emotions you feel, and sit with them without resisting their presence.

Chapter 2: Remind yourself to try and be loving towards yourself and others. Love is not just a feeling; it's a commitment to caring, relating, and being.

- Ex 2.1: Krishnan's RAIN sibling, part 2. Include compassion, ask your emotions what they want to say, and what they need right now. Nurture them.
- Ex 2.2: Mirror work, be kind to yourself.
- Ex 2.3: Use presence exercises to relax yourself to sleep.

- Ex 2.4: Practice behavioral activation. Try to spend 5 minutes doing something you have trouble with. Break the process into itty bitty steps.
- Ex 2.5: Practice gratitude, say a few things you're thankful for today.
- Ex 2.6: Practice listening to somebody for a stretch of time.
- Ex 2.7: Practice loving-kindness meditation.
- Ex 2.8: Engage with your inner child, sit down and talk to them, and meet their needs.

Chapter 3: Notice when your ANTs show up, improve critical thinking, and challenge your negative core beliefs.

- Ex 3.1: Sit down and think of times where you've had trouble. Revisit what you were thinking and identify an ANT. You may do this for several things
- Ex 3.2: Use "I believe I am..." or "I believe others/world is..." prompt to identify negative beliefs.
- Ex 3.3: Categorize your negative beliefs into mental distortions.
- Ex 3.4: Engage in Socratic Dialogue to question a belief. Reframe the belief.
- Ex 3.5: Create your own value system, what is important to you.

Chapter 4: Let yourself express from the deepest places in you. Return to presence with the exercises.

- Ex 4.1: Do your morning pages every day.
- Ex 4.2: Try maintaining a journal of some kind, maybe to process things at the end of a day.
- Ex 4.3: Write letters to people seeking closure, or just to say things you couldn't normally say.
- Ex 4.4: Use writing prompts to write stories or poetry.
- Ex 4.5: Draw and paint uninhibitedly. Analyse the art, talk to it, question it.
- Ex 4.6: Draw and paint a mandala. Speak with it about wholeness.
- Ex 4.7: Make a moodboard for how you feel, or something you want to express.
- Ex 4.8: Meditate on any artwork and analyse it for personal significance.
- Ex 4.9: Sing, just sing from your diaphragm.
- Ex 4.10: Compose some music on BeepBox, or an instrument.
- Ex 4.11: Listen to a piece of music, analyse it.
- Ex 4.12: Dance like no one's watching, girl.
- Ex 4.13: Capture some photographs, and analyse the photographs. Additionally, edit the photograph and see what changes. What story does either photo tell?
- Ex 4.14: Make small home movies. Color grade, add music, write voice-overs.

Chapter 5: Get deep into your internal systems. Listen to what your soul is saying. Get lots of rest.

- Ex 5.1: Try parts work for an emotion that you are feeling right now. Even just sitting with the part is progress.
- Ex 5.2: Maintain a list of the parts you encounter and come back to them when you can. Maintain a relationship.
- Ex 5.3: Analyse a dream that you had recently.
- Ex 5.4: For the same dream, engage with an object through active imagination.
- Ex 5.5: Engage in some shadow work. Think of a quality you despise in others and examine it in your own system.
- Ex 5.6: Journey to the lower world to meet your power animal.
- Ex 5.7: Journey to the upper world to meet a spirit guide.
- Ex 5.8: Journey to the lower world to meet with an elemental, and ask if they have medicine for you.

BIBLIOGRAPHY

These are the list of books that I found useful over the course of my studies in psychology. This was over a long period of time, so I can't even remember if I finished these. Spend some time reading the introductions and see if they speak to you.

- Brach, T. (2003). Radical acceptance: Embracing your life with the heart of a Buddha. Bantam.
- Beck, J. S. (2011). Cognitive behavior therapy: Basics and beyond (2nd ed.). The Guilford Press.
- Cameron, J. (2002). The artist's way: A spiritual path to higher creativity (10th Anniversary ed.). Tarcher/ Putnam.
- Dwoskin, H. (2003). The Sedona method: Your key to lasting happiness, success, peace and emotional well-being. Sedona Press.
- Ingerman, S., & Wesselman, H. (2010). Awakening to the spirit world: The shamanic path of direct revelation. Sounds True.
- Johnson, R. A. (1991). Owning your own shadow: Understanding the dark side of the psyche. HarperOne.
- Jung, C. G. (1964). Man and his symbols. Dell.

- Kennedy, R. (2021). Anxiety Rx: A new prescription for anxiety relief from the doctor who created it. MindRx Inc.
- Neff, K. (2011). Self-compassion: The proven power of being kind to yourself. William Morrow.
- Schwartz, R. C. (2021). No bad parts: Healing trauma and restoring wholeness with the Internal Family Systems model. Sounds True.
- Stahl, S. (2021). The child in you: The breakthrough method for bringing out your authentic self. TarcherPerigee.